26

WATCHMEN RAISE THEIR VOICES

Watchmen Raise Their Voices

A TALLAGHT BOOK OF THEOLOGY

ESSAYS TO MARK THE 150TH ANNIVERSARY
OF THE DOMINICAN HOUSE OF STUDIES
AT TALLAGHT, DUBLIN
(1855-2005)

Edited by
Vivian Boland OP

DOMINICAN PUBLICATIONS
2006

First published (2006) by
Dominican Publications
42 Parnell Square
Dublin I

ISBN 1-871552-98-2

British Library Cataloguing in Publications Data.
A catalogue record for this book is available
from the British Library.

Cover and book design by Bill Bolger
Cover painting,
Crucifixion, by Patrick Pye,
used with permission

Printed by
Leinster Leader, Naas, Co. Kildare, Ireland

ACKNOWLEDGEMENTS

The publishers are grateful to the following
for assistance in preparing this volume

Teresa Crowley
Deirdre Whelan

CONTENTS

FOREWORD

Pat Lucey, OP
Provincial of Ireland

Not only has Tallaght Village changed beyond recognition in the recent past, it has surely changed even more since, and because, the Dominicans arrived in 1855. Due to historical circumstances, young Dominican friars were forced to go abroad for their education before St Mary's, Tallaght, was set up as the studium or house of studies of the Irish Dominican province. With the passing of the Act of Catholic Emancipation in 1829 the Catholic Church was again allowed out onto the footpaths of Ireland. Part of the property of Corpo Santo, Lisbon, where students had gone to study during the Penal Days, was sold, and the proceeds were invested in Tallaght as a centre of formation and education. Since then it has been there that the vast majority of Irish Dominican men learned the ABCs of Dominican life and were prepared for ministry by being formed in philosophy and theology in the Aula Magna and other classrooms.

Among the alumni of the Tallaght studium are numbered Michael Browne, William Barden, Damian Byrne, Conleth Kearns, Leonard Boyle, Senan Crowe and Richard McLoughlin, not to mention the brothers who have contributed to the book you now hold in your hands – and the rest of us. Nor has the Tallaght house of studies been an island of learning: the ripples from its shore have reached the four corners of the earth. The Christian people of Trinidad and Tobago, India, Latin America (including, for example, Argentina, Paraguay, Brazil, Venezuela, Uruguay and Peru), of Australia, New Zealand, India, Iran and many other locations will have heard mention of Tallaght in their liturgical homilies, classroom lectures and sermon stories, from Dominicans who are graduates of the 'College in the Little Village'. Nor has Tallaght Priory lost it academic status since the Province's House of Formative Studies transferred to St Saviour's, Dublin, in the year 2000. It is now the home of The Priory Institute, a centre which continues to provide courses of theology, particularly through a programme of 'distance' learning. It is my wish that, through The Priory Institute, Tallaght will continue to be a seat of learning for the next one hundred and fifty years and more.

We are indebted to Vivian Boland and all concerned in the production of the present publication – including the fourteen alumni of the Tallaght *studium* who have contributed to its production. It is a monument to St Mary's, Tallaght, as a place of learning.

INTRODUCTION

Vivian Boland, OP

Over many years the Dominican students at St Mary's Priory in Tallaght, Dublin, produced an in-house magazine called *The Watchman*. It gave them an opportunity to practise their writing skills on one another before they 'raised their voices' as preachers and teachers in other parts of Ireland and throughout the world. The essays that follow have been written by friars of the Irish Dominican Province to mark the 150th anniversary of the establishment of the Priory at Tallaght. All the contributors studied there and most have also taught there. But all have been teachers elsewhere too, for St Mary's was always a 'missionary college' preparing men to work not only in Ireland but also in Australia, Argentina, Trinidad and Tobago, India, Iran, Rome, Switzerland, Jerusalem, and elsewhere.

The prophets of the Old Testament often describe the preachers of the Word of God as watchmen or sentinels. In Chapter 52 of Isaiah, for example, from which the title of this collection is taken, the ones who announce the joyful news of God's comforting and strengthening presence are compared to watchmen shouting from the city walls that they can see the Lord returning to be with His people. The joy of the New Testament, then, that God is with us in a radically new way, is first experienced and announced by Mary, the mother of Jesus, in whose honour the Tallaght Priory is dedicated. She is a 'watchman of the heart', we might say, contemplating the things she was learning about her Son, and in her visit to Elizabeth, she is the first to bring to others the news of the Word's Incarnation. The news of Emmanuel – that God is with us, that the Word became flesh, that Jesus is our Lord – must now be brought to every dark and bright corner of human life.

The book roughly follows the pattern of keeping watch and speaking up, study and preaching. Gerard Norton writes about the English translations of the Bible in use at Tallaght during the last century and a half, at the same time giving us an idea of what is involved in preparing a critical edition of the Hebrew Bible and worthy translations of it. Wilfrid Harrington introduces the Gospels, explaining what the literary form of a gospel is, saying something about Matthew, Mark, and Luke, and offering some thoughts on the process of the gospels' formation. Thomas Brodie complements this with an account of an alternative understanding of their formation. Jerome Murphy-O'Connor, renowned for his studies of the life of Paul and of the Church at Corinth, writes here about the experience of exile shared by Jesus and Paul when they were children.

St Dominic and the early Dominicans sought to re-enact the way of life experienced by the apostles in the company of Jesus, learning from him and sharing his mission. Liam Walsh, drawing on the theology of Thomas Aquinas, speaks about the prophetic and contemplative aspects of the preacher's task and shows how Christ is the model of the preacher. The works of Meister Eckhart, a younger contemporary of St Thomas, have enjoyed a revival in recent years, and Donagh O'Shea reflects on one of Eckhart's sermons for which a distinction between two kinds of reason is central, a distinction that turns out to be crucial for understanding some of the difficulties preachers face in engaging with contemporary culture. The issue is treated again by Vivian Boland in his chapter on Dominican study, which looks first at traditions about study in the Order and then at challenges and opportunities offered by contemporary developments.

Preaching in practice means talking to people, in a variety of settings and circumstances. The art and craft of preaching are distinguished and analysed by James Donleavy. Philip Gleeson speaks about the homily, the moment of preaching within a liturgy, which is meant to serve the celebration and not dominate it. But he shows how, if the homily remembers its place, it can achieve a great deal.

Situations of affliction, distress, and alienation, when words can seem empty and trite, present great challenges to the preacher, but the news that God is with us is never more needed than in such situations. Benedict Hegarty offers some thoughts from theologians and philosophers about the search for meaning that all human beings share and that supports those to whom people look for words of interpretation and comfort. Paul Murray shows how the words of poetry in particular have a power to comfort and sustain people, even in times of extreme affliction. He reflects on the mysterious but undeniable healing power of beauty in music, art, and poetry.

If the Word is to become flesh in human lives then its grace must illuminate also the structures of our communal lives, the management of our relationships, the guidance of our decisions, and the making of our commitments. Archie Conleth Byrne offers a summary account of the Dominican approach to moral theology, emphasising the themes of grace, virtue, and justice. The final chapters then consider in more detail two aspects of this reflection on justice. Joseph Kavanagh shows how the Church's tradition contains much wisdom about the necessity and limitations of law, considering such themes as the reception of a law and the principle of equity. The collection ends with a chapter by John Harris on recent developments in Church-State relations in Ireland. He shows how theological developments since Vatican II illustrate more clearly than ever how the Church understands the distinct and complementary contributions of Church and State to the progress of humanity.

Some of the obstacles to preaching are inside preachers. These include defects of character, or of wisdom or virtue, that make them unworthy servants. Having spoken enthusiastically about the watchmen in Chapter 52, Isaiah returns to consider them in Chapter 56, with a sombre message that many will regard as still straightforwardly relevant. The prophet notes:

> Our watchmen are all blind: they notice nothing. Dumb watchdogs all, unable to bark, they dream, lie down, and love to sleep. Greedy dogs that are never satisfied, shepherds who know nothing, they all go their own way, each after his own interest' (56:10-11).

Of course we are not asked to believe in the watchmen but only in the One whose presence they point out. As St Paul puts it:

> What then is Apollos? What is Paul? Servants through whom you came to believe, as the Lord assigned to each. I planted, Apollos watered, but God gave the growth. So neither the one who plants nor the one who waters is anything, but only God who gives the growth ... For we are God's servants, working together (1 Corinthians 3:5-7,9a).

I

The Old Testament Words of God

GERARD J. NORTON, OP

THE OLD TESTAMENT WORDS OF GOD

Gerard J. Norton OP

The Bible has been at the centre of the teaching, preaching, and life of the first 150 years of the Tallaght community. This paper considers some English language editions of the Old Testament used during that period, and the texts on which they were based. Addressing the difficulty posed by the adoption of different readings in contemporary English Bibles, the article introduces two relevant current projects with significant Dominican involvement. Much of what is written here is also true in general terms of the New Testament, but we limit ourselves to a consideration of the Old Testament.

Theologians and those who speak of theology sometimes imply that the Bible is a fixed entity, a reference point that provides a constant touchstone for their free-flowing contemplation. At other times one has the impression that the Bible is imagined as a sort of background music to the formulations of the Queen of Sciences. The 1965 Vatican II Constitution on Divine Revelation, *Dei verbum*, speaks of the study of Scripture as 'the soul of theology' (n.24).

The Old Testament has proved somewhat elusive in the past hundred and fifty years. When teachers and preachers turn from the more general summaries ('the Lord brought Israel from Egypt', 'the Psalms are forms of prayer') to the more precise citations on which much theologising has been built, things get much less certain (*e.g.* Job 19:25-6). The differences between the Bibles in circulation have contributed to this uncertainty.

In the early centuries of printing, mass production of identical texts seemed within reach. Certainly it was an improvement on the situation where each individual manuscript added its own characteristic errors and idiosyncrasies to those of the original from which it had been copied. Yet, the reality was not so uniform. As moveable type was assembled and reassembled to print and reprint parts of the biblical text, the goal of identical texts was still far away. Print runs were short, and texts differed from one another in many ways. In the tradition of English language Bibles, a series of Bibles is named for characteristic errors. Two examples of these are the Wicked Bible of 1631 where the word 'not' was omitted from one of the commandments, thereby instructing the reader 'thou shalt commit adultery', and the Scribes' Bible of 1702 which complained that 'printers have persecuted me' at Ps 119:161 where 'princes' is the more usual translation. Although characterising the Bibles concerned, these errors and features of translation are indicative of the many other variations between one Bible and another. The dream of producing identical Bibles only became reality with photography-based methods of book reproduction. Another kind of problem arose there. Such texts, although identical with one another, were not free of error. An example is found in the early printings of the *Jerusalem Bible* of 1966 when the Psalmist at Ps 122:6 enjoins us to 'Pay for peace in Jerusalem, prosperity to your houses, etc.'

For all the faults to be seen, it is true that in the same period the diffusion of the Bible became wider, and more people had access to the text than ever before. Because of the theological consequences of particular texts, and also by reason of the scale of work involved in production of an edition of the Bible, translation projects have tended to be tightly controlled by the various denominational authorities. Particular texts were denominationally linked and widely spread in that denomination. Where a denomination recognised more than one translation in a language group, these translations were often geographically distinct in their usage. The impression of one established biblical text persisted.

Catholic tradition during Tallaght's first century tended to follow a Biblical translation revised with notes in 1750 by Bishop Richard Challoner of London on the basis of the Douay-Rhiems English translation published in 1582 (NT) and 1609-10 (OT). The Douay-Rhiems Old Testament was based on the Latin Vulgate as revised by Popes Sixtus V and Clement VIII, published in 1592.

Pope Pius XII's encyclical *Divino afflante spiritu* (1943) established the texts in the language of composition of the Old Testament, Hebrew, Aramaic and Greek, as the norm for translations. It was possible to consult a series of responsible critical editions of Hebrew texts (the *Biblia Hebraica* series) and of Greek texts such as the Book of Wisdom or the additions to Daniel and Esther (Rahlf's

Septuaginta). These were to become the reference points for the group of translations now undertaken in a Catholic context. There was inevitably a time lapse. No Catholic translation of the Old Testament into English from the original languages had ever been produced. Some students at Tallaght during these years remember scripture study as dominated by corrections to the Douay-Rhiems text. Their memories are well supported by the heavily pencil-annotated volumes from the time.

A century after Tallaght's foundation, another English translation recommended to theology students was that of Monsignor Ronald Knox (NT 1945, OT 1949, complete 1955). Although it is a remarkable piece of work, the project itself was outdated almost before it was published, both in its use of the Vulgate as a base text and in its project to translate the Bible into a 'timeless English'. The title page indicates that the work is issued for 'private use only'.

Despite the attractions of the Knox version, many Catholics, in Tallaght and elsewhere, opted for a text that was translated from the Hebrew/Aramaic/Greek text. They turned to the *Revised Standard Version* of 1952 (the Deuterocanonical texts were added in 1957 as a separate section), well in advance of the publication of the specifically Catholic edition of the *Revised Standard Version* in 1965. The specifically Catholic edition [of 1965] made no changes in the Old Testament text (this was not the case in the New Testament) but integrated the Deuterocanonical texts and books into the text in the order in which they appear in the Vulgate. (The only exception to the Vulgate order were the so-called additions to Esther. They had been moved to the end of the book by Jerome on the ground that they did not occur in the Hebrew. They are restored to their narrative place in the Catholic RSV of 1965.) This *Revised Standard Version* was a product of the English-language Reformed or Protestant tradition that followed the 1611 King James tradition, also known as the *Authorised Version* (AV). That translation was based on the Hebrew text. This *Authorised Version* (AV) had been revised in 1881 (OT) and 1885 (NT) as the *Revised Version* (RV) for European English speakers. A revision intended for American English speakers, the *American Revised Version* (ARV) was published in 1901. The ARV is the ancestor of the *Revised Standard Version*, the ecumenical *Common Bible* (1977) and the *New Revised Standard Version* (1989).

In the RSV, some corrections were made to the text on the basis of ancient translations from the Hebrew, and these corrections are usually indicated in the apparatus. The language was also modernised. The sculpted but flowing quality of the English appealed to many readers. These translations, in keeping with their Reformation forebears, are presented as a stark text with few headings. Since the *Revised Version* of 1885, Hebrew poetic texts have been translated and laid out in a way that emphasised their poetic qualities and distinguished them from prose texts. This causes few problems for most of the Books of Psalms, Job and Proverbs, but the identification of certain parts of the prophetic literature as poetic is more controversial. Introductions and commentaries are not included. Little explicit guidance is given to the reader on the interpretation of the text. Yet, both the poetic layout of the text and the division into sense paragraphs are strong implicit directions for interpretation.

In surveying English translations in use over the past 150 years, it may seem odd to include a revolutionary French translation, the *Bible de Jérusalem* (finished 1955, one-volume edition 1961). It was no surprise that it had an impact on Tallaght, given the deep commitment of the Irish Province to the *Ecole Biblique*, expressed by the number of the brethren who had already been sent to finish their biblical studies there (Thomas Garde, Conleth Kearns, Ailbe Ryan, Richard McLoughlin, Wilfrid Harrington. Others followed: Jerome Murphy-O'Connor, Benedict Hegarty, Thomas Brodie, Gerard Norton, Michael Savage). Yet it is fair to say that the impact of the *Bible de Jérusalem* on biblical studies in Tallaght was a measure of its impact on European biblical studies as a whole.

This French Bible was a new development in Catholic biblical study. The novelties were in the addition of headings, the interpretative layout of poetic and prayer texts, and the provision of extensive introductions to the books, and notes on the text. These notes were principally historical-critical in nature. On occasion references are made to manuscript or versional evidence, but these are not very intelligible. Notes to the Old Testament tend to be very sober in relation to subsequent Christian interpretation (2 Sam 7; Isa 7:14; Ps 22) although there are some exceptions (Gen 3:15). It is fair to comment that the treatment of the text differed from book to book and editor to editor. This could bewilder the attentive reader. An English edition, *The Jerusalem Bible* (1966), was soon published. It followed the same principles. The introductions and notes to the text were translated from the French edition, and the characteristic layout was adopted. The English version of the Bible text was found by many to be a poor translation. Although the text was intended to be a new translation into English from the Hebrew, Aramaic and Greek (the first Catholic translation into English of the Old Testament ever made from these texts), dependence on the French was clear, and in many places the text was considered faulty. [Anybody who wonders how this happened should read the relevant chapters in Anthony Kenny's *A Path from Rome* (London: Sidgewick and Jackson, 1985).] Henry Wansbrough OSB was responsible for preparation of the *New Jerusalem Bible* (1985) in which the main concerns of critics of the *Jerusalem Bible* were addressed. Not alone did the *Jerusalem Bible* reflect the sometimes adventurous text-critical choices of the French edition, but the capricious translation produced a Bible that at many points was without critical foundation.

The *New American Bible* (NT 1941, complete 1970) was also a Catholic initiative although many eminent non-Catholic scholars were invited to participate in the project. The first editions of the New Testament were translations from the Vulgate, but the final complete edition was translated from the original Greek, Hebrew and Aramaic languages. Attention was paid to the text-critical questions raised in *Biblia Hebraica*, the standard edition of the Tiberian Hebrew text, and also to the new material emerging from the discoveries at Qumran. This latter was particularly evident in the books of Samuel, where corrections to the Hebrew text were made on the basis of (then unpublished) Qumran discoveries and the *Septuagint*. The book of Sirach was translated from the newly discovered Hebrew form and, where necessary, the Greek tradition. All previous translations had been from the Greek alone. Not infrequently, throughout the Bible, the order of the lines was changed by the translators. (For nearly fifty years, until the early 1990s, almost the only access to some of the Qumran discoveries was *via* the notes in the *New American Bible*.) In its concern to present translations from texts as close to the original composition as possible, this edition is the counterpart of the *Bible de Jérusalem*, the *Jerusalem Bible*. Although the text was closer to a Hebrew original, the Hebrew text that constituted that original was frequently quite different from that traditionally transmitted and to be found in the *Biblia Hebraica*, the publication of that standard Tiberian Hebrew text. A companion volume identified these places where an alternative Hebrew text was read, but it was of little use to the average reader (*Textual Notes on the New American Bible* Paterson, N.J., 1970).

At the same time as specifically Catholic translations were undertaken, other Christian groups were moved by the spirit of the times to produce translations of the Bible that on the one hand showed the progress in biblical studies of the previous century, and on the other hand responded to readers' concerns for intelligibility. We have noted above the RSV tradition and its ongoing revisions. A complete revision was commissioned in 1974 in order to take concerns about comprehensibility of the language into account, and other issues such as gender inclusiveness. This was known as the *New Revised Standard Version* (NRSV). The principles of the NRSV translators were described in the preface as being 'as literal as possible' in adhering to the ancient texts and only 'as free as necessary' to make the meaning clear in graceful, understandable English. This seemed unexceptional. However, in their concern to maximise gender inclusiveness, many argue that the NRSV ceased to be an accurate translation of the Old Testament. Rome was unenthusiastic and preferred the *New American Bible* or the *Jerusalem Bible* for liturgical use.

The *New English Bible* (NEB, NT 1961, completed 1970) was intended to be an ecumenical translation of the Bible. The Christian Churches of England and Ireland, including the Catholic Church, were represented on the committee that oversaw the project. The translators wished to move away from the traditional notion of 'biblical English'. Two difficulties were found with the final text. First, the break with 'biblical English' was incomplete and inconsistent. Second, in many places conjectural readings in the original languages were used to make the translation more comprehensible. In the latter instance the hand of S. R. Driver seems to have been particularly heavy. The *Revised English Version* (REB) of 1989 was better adapted to reading aloud in public worship, and less dependent on conjectural readings. Brockington published a volume identifying the different textual choices of the editors, but this was inadequate (L.H. Brockington, *The Hebrew Text of the Old Testament: Readings Adopted by the Translators of the New English Bible*, Oxford University Press, 1973).

Another family of English translations is clustered around *The Living Bible* (NT 1967, completed 1971). These include *Reach out* (1969), *The Way* (1972, with a Catholic version in 1973), and *The New Living Translation* (1996). This is a paraphrase of the *American Standard Version* of 1901 and was originally intended to make that Bible more comprehensible for children. The proceeds from the vast sales of these volumes enabled the foundation of Tyndale House publishers, whose publications tend to be seen, from a Catholic point of view, as evangelical.

Other editions too made their mark. The frequently scorned *Good News Bible* (1976), earlier known as *Good News For Modern Man* (1966, later editions 1967 and 1971) and also sold as *Today's English Version*, was devised to be 'natural, clear, simple and unambiguous' as it says in its preface. Stupendous line drawings by Annie Vallotton made a badly-bound paperback on poor quality paper a thing of beauty, even of art. This Bible also established 'dynamic equivalence' as a translation issue for the Bible. That is to say, clarity of meaning is emphasised more than literary form, and the translation aims to produce the same effect as the original had on its readers. Little attempt is made to establish a text other than that provided by the 1937 *Biblia Hebraica*, or Rahlf's *Septuagint* for the Deuterocanonical volumes.

Recently the *Christian Community Bible* has been well received in the Irish Church. Its scholarship and notes reflect its Filipino context. Like the *Jerusalem Bible*, it is translated from the original Hebrew, Aramaic and Greek, and is accompanied by notes, chronologies, a lexicon, and even a chart indicating the readings for Mass in the liturgical cycle. Unlike the *Jerusalem Bible* it gives little or no indication that the Hebrew text is problematic in places. There is no note indicating where it has adopted a text other than the *Biblia Hebraica*, whether the translator has been moved to conjecture an interpretation of the Hebrew, or a different Hebrew text, or simply to accept readings of ancient texts other than the *Biblia Hebraica*. It is a self-conscious presentation of the Bible in the context of a living Christian tradition. The introductions and notes do not shirk the problems caused by aspects of that tradition that have been dominated by Western white males. The text is presented in a way that shows the translators' understanding of the composition history of the text. The extensive notes are more explicitly Christian and homiletic than those of the *Jerusalem* or other contemporary annotated English Bibles.

What is the effect on the Catholic, indeed the Christian, community of this variety of Bibles? On the one hand it risks diminishing the confidence of the faithful in the dependability of the Bible. It can be difficult for people when they feel that whenever they cite a text of the Bible, it can be undermined by a citation from a different translation. The differences between translations are by no means restricted to the issue of synonyms. Even that would be difficult, for usage admits of few real synonyms.

It is clear that the dream of unity that might have followed Pope Pius XII's embrace (in his 1943 encyclical *Divino afflante spiritu*) of the original languages as the proper source for translations has not yet become reality. On the one hand this was because of the variety of translation features that came into use as modern translations were made with particular readerships in mind. On the other hand, the base text for each of these translations was different. The emphasis of *Divino afflante spiritu* on the study of texts in the original languages and the desire that this be combined with a real skill in literary criticism of the same text (n° 16) was combined with a confidence in the objectivity of the rules of textual criticism (n° 18). The apparent monolithic unity of the Hebrew and Aramaic Bible dissipated before the textual plurality revealed in discoveries at Qumran and around the Dead Sea. These began in the same decade as Pius XII's charter. Texts that were ancestors to the received Tiberian text of *Biblia Hebraica* were found at Qumran. Other texts were found whose place in the transmission was not so clear. It was plausibly argued that in some cases the earliest witness to a text composed in Hebrew (Jeremiah) was in fact to be found in Greek. These discoveries confirmed that there was a plurality of texts in use by Jews (and hence Christians) in the time of Jesus and the first Christians. As a result the encyclical of Pius XII seemed to provide fewer answers. What text constituted the original, from which translations should be made? The rules of textual and literary criticism of the Hebrew Bible had to be revised, if not rewritten. Although it made sense to place weight on the texts in their original languages, the state of the texts that have formed the basis of our standard editions, that is, their relationship to the original composition by a prophet or other writer, is now less clear than it seemed in 1943.

Complex questions concerning canon also arose in the wake of the Qumran discoveries. The stabilisation of the Jewish canon as witnessed in the great tenth-century manuscript on which our editions of the Hebrew Bible are based, was now seen to be much later than had previously been thought. Why should Christians, whose ancestors had already broken with Judaism at the time of the formation of the Jewish Canon, continue to give it weight?

It is interesting that just as we have the technical capacity to produce for the first time an indefinite number of identical Bibles, the number of different Bibles being produced has mushroomed. This has led to a situation reminiscent of the Early Church when several Greek translations of the Hebrew text, some aspiring to be more literal, others to be more literary, co-existed. In this third-century context Origen assembled his great work, the *Hexapla*. This provided a rich resource for Christian theologians. They seem to have revelled in the variety of the translations allowed, without particular preference for any particular one. (See M. Harl, 'La Septante et la pluralité textuelle des Ecritures: le témoignage des Pères grecs' *La Langue de Japhet* Paris: Cerf, 1994, pp.253-266.) One might paraphrase the situation thus: if a Hebrew text can mean either A or B, does it have to mean A and not B or B and not A? The translator often has to make a choice. Can both interpretations be allowed? The latter seems to have been the stance of the Church Fathers who used the *Hexapla*. The existence of multiple translations in Greek allowed a fertile multiplicity of interpretations. Can the multiplicity of texts be seen in the same positive light today?

Some confusion has been caused by the publication of a new edition of a Latin text of the Bible, the *Nova Vulgata* (completed in 1979), and by subsequent Roman pronouncements in its regard, in particular the 2001 instruction *Liturgiam authenticam*, on article 36 of the 1963 Vatican II Constitution on the Sacred Liturgy (*Sacrosanctum concilium*). For some, this represents a call to turn from confusing multiplicity, and adhere rather to the clarity of a single official text. This New Vulgate was prepared on the instructions of Paul VI, and was originally intended to provide an improved Latin text for the reformed Latin liturgy. The authority of the Vulgate (sometimes seen as transferred to this *Nova Vulgata*) was clearly and magisterially interpreted at the Council of Trent, and further by Pius XII in *Divino afflante spiritu* n° 21, and again by the Second Vatican Council's Dogmatic Constitution *Dei Verbum* n° 22. Somewhat unexpectedly, the vernacular liturgy was in place before the completion of this New Vulgate. As a result the role of this text was more restricted than intended. It continues to be of relevance in Latin Church documents and some other contexts.

The situation was complicated by what seemed like an insistence in *Liturgiam authenticam* n°s 37, 41 and 43, that the *Nova Vulgata* was an *editio typica*, in the sense that other translations were to bow to its authority. Richard Clifford has demonstrated on the contrary that the sense in which the *Nova Vulgata* was to be seen as an *editio typica* was to be understood as requiring the text of the 1979 edition from the Libreria Editrice Vaticana to be followed exactly in further printings of the liturgical Latin text. This is to be distinguished from the use of the same phrase '*editio typica*' when it is used with reference to liturgical texts. (See Richard J. Clifford S.J. 'The Authority of the *Nova Vulgata*: A Note on a Recent Roman Document', *Catholic Biblical Quarterly* 63 (2001) pp. 197-202.) In short, then, neither the publication of the *Nova Vulgata*, nor the interpretation of its authority by *Liturgiam authenticam*, affects the deep commitment of the Catholic Church to respect the truth of the situation where there is a divergence between ancient readings in the languages of composition of the Bible, or indeed where a text allows of more than one interpretation.

The notes above indicate that the English translations in common use were not made from a single base text. The translators used alternative readings from the versions, and conjectures based on philological premises. The situation was exaggerated in poetic books where the text was often altered to make it comply with the critic's notion of proper Hebrew poetry, and the translation of poetic aspects sometimes took priority over strict philological accuracy. In no English translation of the Old Testament currently in use can the options taken by the translators be said to be comprehensively indicated to the reader.

In this context, those translating the Bible into languages where there was no existing biblical translation, often in missionary contexts, were frequently at a loss. This was the case even if they were competent in Hebrew and Aramaic. At least five thousand of the differences between current scholarly translations reflect different choices of base text made by the translators. Many more differences represent translation choices. How is the reader to tell the difference? When different base readings were adopted by the scholarly modern translations, which reading represented the text that should best be translated into another language?

This was the background to the long research of Dominique Barthélemy OP and his colleagues in the Hebrew Old Testament Text Project (HOTTP) of the United Bible Societies. They examined 5,000 cases in the Old Testament where significant differences in selected scholarly biblical translations were based on different choices of readings in the Hebrew Bible. These five thousand readings did not include cases where the differences between translations were based on different interpretations of the same Hebrew text whether these were philological, or determined by concerns for translation principles such as dynamic equivalence or gender inclusiveness. This project led to a four-stage analysis of the history of the Hebrew Bible, and a recognition that for each book there was an 'earliest attested text' that is the limit to which responsible textual criticism can go on the basis of the available evidence. In most books of the Old Testament – Daniel is an exception – this earliest attested text was much later than the supposed date of composition of the text.

A concern to present the evidence clearly and appropriately underlies the publication of *Biblia Hebraica Quinta* (2004-). The editors, under the leadership of Adrian Schenker OP of Fribourg, are inspired in many respects by the work of the HOTTP. They explicitly resist the temptation to create an eclectic text that would itself represent the earliest attainable reading in each case. The time is not yet ripe for that. Instead, as a step towards this end, the text of the earliest surviving complete manuscript is presented in its entirety (the base manuscript). Where readings in the ancient translations may arguably present a Hebrew text other than that of the base manuscript, all the relevant translations and texts are presented and their evidence weighed in a critical apparatus. Conjectures, when included in the discussion, are clearly identified. Through reading the critical apparatus, then, the reader may find indications of where a textual option in the tradition of the base manuscript could be replaced by another, on grounds that it is earlier. A second volume of commentary on the critical apparatus gives the grounds on which the editor has made this suggestion.

Leaving the matter there would not do justice to the evidence. In some cases the ancient versions differ from the base text, but it is not simply a matter of one reading having been substituted for another, whether by error or intent. Rather it is the case that two or more literary forms of a text have been handed down to us. This phenomenon should hardly surprise readers of the first chapters of Genesis, or of Samuel and Chronicles, or indeed Exodus 20 and Deuteronomy 5. [We keep here to Old Testament examples, but of course the Synoptic Gospels provide food for similar reflection.] The Hebrew and Greek forms of Jeremiah are a case in point, as indeed are the Hebrew and Greek Esther and Daniel as well as part of Samuel.

The difference between all these examples just given and the different literary forms of, say, Jeremiah, are that in the former cases both literary forms were accepted into the Canon whereas in the case of Jeremiah one form is in the Septuagint (and daughter translations) and the other form is in the Hebrew text. The form considered basic depends on the canon being followed. The Greek text provides the background to much patristic theology that was formative for both Western and Eastern Churches and continues to be the canonical text of the Eastern Churches. The option for the Hebrew text as base is linked with the name of Jerome, and the options taken in his translation that was to become the Vulgate. For some books extant in two literary forms, the discussion of which of these forms may have derived from the other or whether they both derived from a third (lost) form remains lively. It would not be logical to combine those two ancient literary forms to produce a new modern text that may never before have existed. The editors of *Biblia Hebraica Quinta* edit a text from the Jewish tradition, but indicate divergent literary traditions, and signal that they should not be combined to form a new text. In this way the integrity of an edition of the Hebrew Bible is maintained, but the decisions for the Christian community remain.

Another Vatican document, *The Interpretation of the Bible in the Church*, was prepared by the Pontifical Biblical Commission, and published by the Vatican in 1993, marking fifty years since Pius XII's *Divino afflante spiritu*. This document is unusual in the sequence of Roman documents dealing with the Word of God and its interpretation, in that it passes in review a number of methods of interpretation currently in wide use in biblical studies. Textual criticism is passed over fairly lightly, without much consideration of the interplay between textual and literary criticism. At the beginning of the document, the Commission distinguishes methods (a group of scientific procedures employed in order to explain texts) from approaches (a question of an inquiry proceeding from a particular point of view). The document receives many modern methods and approaches warmly, but also integrates broader hermeneutical questions, with due respect to the fathers of the Church reading the Bible theologically in the heart of a living tradition (section III.B.2).

What we have just said about the *Biblia Hebraica Quinta* indicates that of itself it cannot function simply as the Christian Old Testament. It tries to present a large part of that tradition well, but is not itself the complete tradition. Coincidentally, perhaps, a new project of the *Ecole Biblique* in Jerusalem is born of similar concerns. The *Ecole Biblique* had previously been responsible for the *Bible de Jérusalem*. This new project is carefully named *La Bible en ses Traditions*. The initiators of the project are aware of the differing literary forms of certain texts. They are also aware of the different interpretations that texts have had over long centuries of Christian and Jewish tradition, and that some texts have sparked off rich Christian reflection even though the feature of the text at issue may be far from what would now be considered the earliest historical meaning of the text. The historical critical quest encouraged by Pius XII had to take its place among the great variety of ways in which the texts had been interpreted throughout history, influencing Christian and Jewish thought.

Our witnesses to the history of interpretation come only in part from the translations that were made. In ancient or modern times, they determine the meaning of the text for communities, particularly for those whose capacity to read the 'original' text is limited. Although the interpretations given by the first communities were important, so also were the interpretations of Jerome, Thomas, and Luther (not to mention Rashi, Ibn Ezra, and others of the great Jewish tradition, often ignored by Christians). The current stage of the *Ecole Biblique* project envisages a presentation of the text that will be similar to that of the Talmud, where commentaries are grouped around the primary text, itself situated in the centre of the page. In the Christian tradition, this recalls the presentation of the *Postillae litterales* on the whole Bible of Nicholas of Lyra in the fourteenth century, perhaps the finest representation of reading the Bible as a glossed text, a phenomenon that was the norm in the Middle Ages. This was also the kind of layout found in the first printed Rabbinical Hebrew Bibles of 1516/17 and 1524/25 printed by Daniel Bomberg, and often reproduced to the present day in Jewish contexts.

La Bible en ses Traditions was presented in this way in the informal publication of *Nouvelles de Jérusalem* of 2000:

> The idea (it is too early to speak of a precise plan) is to build upon the existing *BdeJ* by highlighting how the Bible was received within the tradition(s) of the church. In essence this would involve two changes in the format of the *BdeJ*. Important variant readings, which have given rise to alternative theological interpretations, would be displayed in synoptic form within the text, rather than in footnotes. The footnotes would be split into two parts. In addition to refined

and updated historico-critical notes, there would be a new level for the interpretative traditions, which in the OT would focus on typology, and in the NT on Christology. The marginal references would be focused less on material parallels and more on interpretation. The idea is not to produce another reference book ... , the problem is no longer accessibility, but relevance. What is really important? Our ambition is to distil the essential necessary for a cultivated, modern appreciation of the message of the Bible into a one-volume translation. The project itself is expected to last at least until 2018.

CONCLUSION

When we deal with the Biblical text, we must recognise that we do not yet have the original text of the biblical author and in many cases we do not know how this relates to the earliest attainable text in the original languages. Integrity requires of us that we acknowledge the complexity of the situation. The texts of the Bible exhibit a rich pluriformity. It takes courage to recognise and live with this. Awareness of this many-textured nature of the Old Testament has always contributed to the rich history of its interpretation. We do the Word of God a disservice if we do not recognise, and indeed relish, the variety of texts in the original languages and the diversity of influential interpretations and translations that have shaped, and continue to shape, our Christian tradition.

BIBLIOGRAPHY OF PRINCIPAL WORKS REFERRED TO

Biblia Hebraica ...edidit Rud. Kittel. Stuttgart: Württembergische Bibelanstalt, 1937 (known as BHK.)

Biblia Hebraica Stuttgartensia ...ediderunt K. Elliger et W.Rudolph. Stuttgart: Deutsche Bibelgesellschaft 1967/77 (known as BHS).

Biblia Hebraica Quinta Editione cum apparatu critico novis curis elaborato . . . communiter ediderunt A.Schenker (praeses), Y.A.P. Goldman, A. van der Kooij, G. J. Norton, S. Pisano, J de Waard, R.D. Weis. Stuttgart: Deutsche Bibelgesellschaft, 2004ff (known as BHQ).

Christian Community Bible: Complete text translated from the original languages with introductions and commentaries for the Christian Communities and those who seek God. First edition 1971. 30th edition Quezon City: St Paul's 2000

Clifford, Richard J. 'The Authority of the *Nova Vulgata*: a note on a recent Roman document, *Catholic Biblical Quarterly*, 63 (2001) pp.197-202.

Divino afflante spiritu, an Encyclical letter of Pope Pius XII. Original in *Acta Apostolica Sedis* 35 (1943) 297-326. Translation in *Rome and the Study of Scripture* St Meinrad, Indiana, 7th edition 1964.

Douay Rhiems-Challoner. The Holy Bible translated from the Latin Vulgate and diligently compared with other editions in divers languages (Douai, A.D. 1609; Rheims, A.D.1582) published as revised and annotated by Authority, with a preface by the Cardinal Archbishop of Westminster. This edition contains Bishop Challoner's notes, newly compiled indices, tables, and verified references. Also Leo XIII's Encyclical on the Study of the Holy Scriptures (*Providentissimus Deus*). London: Burns Oates and Washbourne, 1914.

Good news Bible = Good news for Modern Man = Today's English Version New York: American Bible Society, 1966ff.

Harl, Marguerite. *La Langue de Japhet*. Paris: Cerf, 1994.

Knox, Ronald A. *The New Testament of our Lord and Saviour Jesus Christ* : newly translated from the Latin Vulgate and authorized by the Archbishops and Bishops of England and Wales. London: Burns, Oates and Washbourne, 1945

The Old Testament : newly translated from the Latin Vulgate by Ronald A. Knox at the request of the Cardinal Archbishop of Westminster. 2 vols. London: Burns, Oates and Washbourne, 1949

La Bible de Jérusalem: La Sainte Bible traduite en français sous la direction de l'Ecole biblique de Jérusalem. Paris: Cerf, 1961.

Liturgiam authenticam: on the use of vernacular languages in the publication of the books of the Roman liturgy. Fifth instruction 'for the right implementation of the Constitution on the Sacred Liturgy of the Second Vatican Council'. Rome: Congregation for Divine Worship and the Discipline of the Sacraments. 2001.

New English Bible Oxford/Cambridge University Press, 1970

Nova Vulgata - Bibliorum Sacrorum Editio sacrosanti oeucumenici concilii Vaticanii II ratione habita iussu Paulii PP. VI recognita auctoritate Ionnis Pauli PP. II promulgata editio typica altera. Constitutio Apostolica Praefatio ad Lectorem Praenotanda Vetus Testamentum Novum Testamentum Appendix Rome: 1986 (first edition 1979; there are few differences of any consequence between the editions.)

Pontifical Biblical Commission, 'The Interpretation of the Bible in the Church' (1993); *Origins* 23, no. 29 (6 January 1994), pp. 498-524; also printed as a booklet by St Paul Books and Media, Boston. Also found as Joseph F. Fitzmyer The Biblical Commission's Document "The Interpretation of the Bible in the Church" : Text and Commentary (*Subsidia Biblica* – 18) Rome: Biblical Institute Press, 1995.

Septuaginta. Id est Vetus Testamentum graece iuxta LXX interpretes. 2 vols, Stuttgart: Württembergische Bibelanstalt, 1935.

Textual Notes on the New American Bible, Paterson N.J.: St Anthony's Guild 1970.

The Holy Bible: Revised Standard Version, containing the Old and New Testaments. Catholic Edition, prepared by the Catholic Biblical Association of Great Britain. With a foreword by His Eminence Cardinal John Heenan Archbishop of Westminster. London: Catholic Truth Society. 1966.

The Jerusalem Bible, London: Darton, Longman and Todd 1966.

The New American Bible (St Joseph Edition) / translated from the original languages, with critical use of all the ancient sources by members of the Catholic Biblical Association of America; sponsored by the Bishop's Committee of the Confraternity of Christian Doctrine. New York: Catholic Book Publishing Co., 1970.

The Revised English Bible with the Apocrypha, Oxford / Cambridge University Press, 1989.

The Way: Catholic edition. An illustrated edition of the Living Bible as developed by the editors of Campus Life Magazine, Youth for Christ International. London: Coverdale House,1972

Vatican Council II : the Conciliar and Post-Conciliar Documents. General editor, Austin Flannery. Dublin: Dominican Publications, 1975.

II

Gospel and Gospels

WILFRID HARRINGTON, OP

GOSPEL AND GOSPELS

Wilfrid J. Harrington, OP

There is only so much one can reasonably hope to cover in a single article. It is difficult enough to treat meaningfully of the three Synoptic Gospels in short compass. An attempt to fit in, as well, the distinctively different Fourth Gospel, would be unrealisitc. Our modest concern here is the Gospel genre and an assessment of the Synoptics.

GOSPEL

Gospel is not a wholly distinctive literary form. It belongs to a broad Greco-Roman genre of *bioi* – lives – or, more specifically, historical 'lives'. The purpose of a *bios* was, above all, to bring out clearly the nature of the subject. A Gospel, as a *bios Iesou*, highlights the uniqueness of Jesus in terms of christology. Our Gospels are a mixture of narrative and discourse, centred on the person, life and teaching of Jesus of Nazareth, with special interest in his death and resurrection. All four evangelists were concerned to set out both the *story* of Jesus and also what they took to be the *significance* of his actions and teaching. He is the focus; he gives meaning to all.

A gospel is not objective biography. This story is shot through with resurrection faith. A gospel is written for believers: it is a Christian document addressed to Christians. More specifically, each gospel was, in the first place, written for a particular Christian community and with the needs of that community firmly in mind. The evangelists presented the 'facts' with the intention of bringing out the meaning which the events held for those who encountered them. They set out to voice the faith of the early Church. The nucleus of that faith is that the crucified Jesus had been raised from the dead.

The fourth evangelist has given us the aim of an evangelist. His selective presentation of the 'signs' of Jesus was in order that the Christian disciple might go on believing that the historical person, Jesus, is the Messiah of Jewish expectation, that he is the Son of

God. He wrote so that, through their deepened faith in Jesus Christ, Christians might find life in him and live that life to the full (Jn 20:31). In other words, his concern was christology and discipleship.

The gospels are proclamations of the Good News. They are aimed at Christians striving to live the Christian Way.

PLOT AND CHARACTERS

A gospel, addressed to a Christian community, has the concerns and needs of the community in mind. These are concerns and needs perceived by the *evangelist* (not necessarily by the recipients or not by all of them). His readers know the basic story as well as the author does. He makes his point by telling the story in his manner. Each of the evangelists tells the same story (this is manifestly true of the Synoptists), but the emphases of the gospels differ considerably. The events and actions of a story, the plot, regularly involve conflict; indeed, conflict (not necessarily violent conflict) is the heart of story. Not alone do the gospels have a plot, but the plot is – in a sense – the evangelist's interpretation of the story. As writers of narrative literature, the evangelists achieve their purpose by means of plot and characterisation.

Characterisation refers to the manner in which a narrator brings characters to life in a story. In literary terms, 'characters' are not the same as persons. In day-to-day life we know one another imperfectly. I may guess at your thoughts; I cannot really know what you are thinking. Characters can be transparent. The narrator may expose a character fully to the reader, can permit the reader to get inside the character. Alternatively, one can present a 'true' picture of any character, or characters, and make them known to us more intimately than they, as persons, were in fact known to their contemporaries.

The distinction between 'character' and 'person' is important. Jesus of Nazareth was a wholly historical person. He was a first-century Palestinian Jew who carried out what – he was convinced – was a God-given mission to his people. He was rejected, and was condemned and executed by an alliance of Jewish religious and Roman political authorities. The 'character' Jesus of the Gospels is this Jesus now viewed through Christian eyes, seen through the prism of 'resurrection-faith'. Each gospel has several characters, of varying importance for the flow of the story. Jesus carries the central message of each gospel. And Jesus is the chief spokesman of an evangelist's concern.

THE SOURCES

Like the Old Testament prophets, Jesus was a preacher, not a writer. And, besides, the earliest proclamation of the Good News would have been oral. At some stage, likely quite early, written texts would have appeared. This would not have spelled the end of oral transmission. The existence of sources is explicitly noted by Luke: 'Many have undertaken to set down an orderly account of the events that have been fulfilled among us' (Lk 1:1). It is evident that Matthew and Luke used sources, and literary sources at that.

The great majority of New Testament scholars work with the Two-Document Hypothesis: Mark is our earliest gospel; Matthew and Luke have used Mark and another hypothetical text known as Q (from the German *Quelle*, 'source'). The theory accounts, very reasonably, for the large amount of gospel material shared by Matthew and Luke. In addition, each of these two has material proper to himself (designated 'M' and 'L').

The source Q, a Greek document, was, arguably, in the main, a collection of sayings and parables. The outline of it is found, most persuasively, in Luke. It is strongly sapiential in tone and carries a notable eschatological emphasis. Of course, the hypothetical Q document is not extant. This has not hindered some from presenting assured reconstructions. Nor, indeed, from describing the Q community, with a confident sketch of its theology. The existence of a Q document is the hypothesis that best explains the remarkable non-Marcan connections between Matthew and Luke. But that shadowy Q should be left in its decent anonymity.

The reality of gospel growth may have been more complex. Yet, in its broad lines, the Two-Document Hypothesis has served us well in our study of the gospels.

MARK: THE TRIUMPH OF FAILURE

Underestimated from early times because of its brevity (almost all of Mark is found in Matthew and Luke), the gospel of Mark has, in our day, come into its own. Above all, the evangelist Mark stands side-by-side with Paul as a stalwart proclaimer of a theology of the cross – *theologia crucis*. And, congenial to modern christology, the Marcan Jesus is the most human in the gospels. The Gospel according to Mark sets the pattern of a gospel: it is concerned with christology and discipleship. Jesus is the Son of God, that is, God-appointed leader of the new covenant people; he is 'son of man', the human one who came to serve, the one faithful unto death. A person who has come to terms with the cross (with the meaning of his death) can know him and can confess him – like the centurion (Mk 15:39). His disciples did not understand him before Calvary. The Christian reader of the first century, and of today, is being challenged to come to terms with the love of God shown forth in the cross of Jesus.

THE SETTING OF MARK

The view that Mark had written in Rome about 65 CE and for people in Rome, had long been the prevalent one. But it has not gone unchallenged, because the traditional data that point to this provenance and date are of uncertain worth. We are forced back to the text of the gospel: to an anonymous writing of the first Christian century. The author is not named in the gospel; the traditional name 'Mark' was quite common. Nothing in the gospel points necessarily to a Roman origin. We can be sure that 'Mark' wrote for a specific community and in face of the actual circumstances of that community. We are left to tease out a plausible setting for his gospel, and a likely date for its being written.

Today we confidently set the writing of the gospel close to the events of the Jewish war of 66-70 CE. A careful reading of Mark 13 would suggest a date soon after the Roman destruction of Jerusalem in 70 CE. Together with mounting scholarly opinion, I would propose that Mark was written to and for a Christian community somewhere in the Roman province of Syria. This would offer a setting close to the tragic events of the war. The community may even have harboured Christian refugees from the conflict, making it that much more immediate.

The Gospel of Mark, after an introduction (1:1-13) which sets the stage for the drama that follows, is built up of two complementary parts. The first (1:14-8:30) is concerned with the mystery of Jesus' identity; it is dominated by the question 'who is Jesus?' The emphasis in this part of Mark is on Jesus' miracles; the teaching is largely parabolic. The second part (8:31-16:8) is concerned with the messianic destiny of Jesus: a way of suffering and death. The emphasis in this second half of Mark is on Jesus' teaching which, now directed at his disciples, builds upon their acknowledgment of him as Messiah. It is concerned mainly with the nature of his messiahship and with the suffering it will entail both for himself and for his followers.

THE GOSPEL AND THE MAN

'Who then is this?' (4:41). The question was wrung from the awestruck disciples of Jesus when, at his word, a great calm had fallen upon the troubled waters and their storm-tossed boat had come to rest. For Mark, that chastened crew might have been the community, the little church, for whom he wrote. He wrote for people such as those who needed to know Jesus, who wanted to understand who he really was. He wrote for Christians who doubted and were fearful: 'Teacher, do you not care if we perish?' (v 38). He wrote for Christians who did not relish the idea of being disciples of a suffering Messiah. He wrote for Christians very like ourselves. His gospel is a tract for our time.

We may ask, what of Mark? His gospel shows him to be a storyteller of great natural talent, a man with an eye for telling detail, a man who could effectively structure his material. Mark emerges, too, as a theologian of stature. Some have argued for a Pauline influence on Mark. Whatever about that, the Christ of Mark is a Christ whom Paul would recognise, and the Gospel of Mark is one that Paul would not have disdained to call his own. Mark's gospel is the gospel of Jesus Christ, the 'Son of God', and closes with the resounding declaration: 'Truly, this man was God's Son!' And yet, his Jesus is a man who was indignant and angry, who took children into his arms, a man who suffered and died. This Son of Man who came 'not to be served but to serve, and to give his life as a ransom for many' (10:45) is the Christ whom Paul preached: 'When I came to you, brothers and sisters, I did not come proclaiming the mystery of God to you in lofty words or wisdom. For I decided to know nothing among you except Jesus

Christ, and him crucified' (1 Cor 2:1-2). Paul the apostle, the first great Christian theologian, had come to terms with the scandal of the cross. Mark the evangelist is, perhaps, the next notable Christian theologian in line.

FAILURE

The story of Jesus, as told in Mark, is a story of human failure: the failure of Israel, failure of the disciples, the seeming failure of Jesus himself. Yet, Jesus, the Son, won through to 'resurrection life' by his openness to the ways of God. Faithfulness to God led him to acceptance of death on the cross, thereby becoming Messiah and Son of God.

In his ministry Jesus sought to draw others into a following of this way. Failure of the disciples reached its climax in their flight at the arrest of Jesus (14:50). It seemed that women disciples had redeemed the situation. They, albeit at a distance, witnessed the crucifixion (15:40), saw where the body had been laid (15:47) and, later, came to anoint it (16:1). Assured that Jesus had been raised (16:6) they were commanded to take the Easter message to the failed disciples (16:7). Mark has the last, unexpected, word: 'So they went out and fled from the tomb, for terror and amazement seized them; and they said nothing to any one, for they were afraid' (16:8). At the last the women join the men disciples in failure, sharing their fear and flight.

In the end, all human beings fail. God alone succeeds. The Father had not abandoned the Son (15:34) but had raised Jesus from the dead (16:6). The failed disciples will encounter the risen Lord in Galilee (14:28; 16:7), not because they have succeeded, but solely because of the initiative of God. Fulfilment of the promise of 14:28; 16:7 is not in the text of Mark's gospel. It is in the Christian community that received the story.

> The conclusion of Mark's Gospel is not a message of failure but a resounding affirmation of God's design to overcome all imaginable human failure (16:1-8) in and through the action of God's beloved Son (1:1-13). The words addressed to the struggling disciples at the Transfiguration are addressed to all who take up this gospel: "Listen to him" (9:7).[1]

1. Francis J. Moloney, *The Gospel of Mark*, A Commentary, Peabody, MA, Hendrickson, 2002, p.354

MATTHEW: THE MEASURE OF WISDOM

In the decade 80-90 CE a Jewish Christian theologian – we name him 'Matthew' – made a synthesis of Mark and Q. He had, besides, access to other material (conventionally designated 'M'). His community, based likely at Antioch in Syria, was in a crisis situation. It had been a wholly Jewish community, tolerated within Judaism. But now, after the destruction of Jerusalem in 70 CE, and the reorganisation of a shattered Judaism, it had broken with official Judaism. As a Jewish Christian, writing out of and for a Jewish Christian community, Matthew, like all Jews, had to face up to a radical challenge to Jewish identity. There were stark questions: Where is Israel now? Who is heir to the biblical promises?

The Jewish Christian, Matthew, wrote a Christian gospel. For him, as for Paul, the hope of Israel was in Jesus Christ. His post-70 CE situation was not that of Paul. The Apostle was wholly convinced that Israel had not been set aside, because it never could be (cf Romans 9-11). Matthew, immersed in the conflict situation after 70 CE, was not so sanguine. For him, official Judaism was the enemy. His polemical stance is understandable in the context of his situation. Taken out of context, it has proved disastrous. His Chapter 23, above all, has led to a practically universal Christian characterisation of Pharisees as 'hypocrites' – grossly unfair. And that seeming self-curse, 'his blood be on us and on our children' (27:25), has occasioned brutal persecution of Jews throughout Christian history. There has been a sad failing in perception. In Matthew's situation ethnic Jews, Christian and non-Christian, were in conflict. There was no love lost. But this was not anti-Semitism.

PHARISEES AND SCRIBES

The Pharisees formed a religious and political grouping of devout Jews who perceived a threat to the very existence of Jews as a distinct ethnic, cultural and religious entity. They emphasised detailed study and observance of the Law of Moses. Besides, they possessed a normative body of tradition – the traditions of the 'fathers' or 'elders'. As a major religious force, they enjoyed the respect of the people. All four gospels attest to frequent contact of Jesus with Pharisees throughout the ministry. This relationship was, not surprisingly, one of tension because he and they addressed the same constituency. He and they sought to influence the main body of Palestinian Jews and win them over to their respective visions of what God was calling Israel to be. It is noteworthy that Pharisees are practically absent from all gospel passion narratives. The death of Jesus was brought about, not by Pharisees, but by a religious and political alliance of 'Jerusalem priesthood' and Roman political authority.

As for the scribes, Palestinian scribes in Jesus' time were, in fact, bureaucrats. That they were a distinct religious group with an acknowledged power base is simply not the case.

Matthew pairs scribes and Pharisees without regard for differences. For him 'scribes and Pharisees' represent the opposition: official Judaism ranged against his Christian community. The phrase also embraces a tendency within his Christian community. Conflict between the Jewish authorities and Jesus is well documented in the gospels, but Matthew 23 is something special. As it stands, it is an indictment of Pharisaic Judaism, painfully reflecting the bitter estrangement of church and synagogue towards the close of the first century CE. At the same time, Matthew instances 'scribes and Pharisees' as the negative side of Christian leadership: 'Jesus said to the crowds *and to his disciples*' (23:1). In 23:1-7 Jesus castigates Pharisees and scribes in the third person – 'they'. Then, in 23:8-12, he changes to the second person – 'you': he addresses the church. We observe an ironical twist in Matthew's graphic narrative of Jesus' denunciation of those in authority in the synagogue. He is concerned that, in his day, Jesus' followers have developed attitudes and behaviour reminiscent of those Pharisees and scribes. In depicting Jesus' staunch rejection of such conduct, he unmasks the problematic character of leadership in Christian communities.

THE STRUCTURE

The centre of the gospel – the public ministry – is built up of five major sections, each with a pattern of narrative-plus-discourse (Chapters 3-25). To this, the Infancy Narrative is prologue or introduction, the Passion Narrative conclusion or climax. However one seeks to structure it, this gospel is, before anything else, a proclamation of Jesus of Nazareth, *risen* Lord, present and active in the Christian community. Matthew acknowledged Jesus as Prophet and Healer. What, in our respect, marks him off from the other Synoptists is his emphasis on Jesus as Teacher or Sage. In the stressful days after the traumatic disaster of 70 CE, Matthew's community found itself in a state of 'cold war' with official Judaism. Its stance is that Jesus is the Teacher who speaks more authoritatively than Moses. This is stressed by Matthew. Arguably, the statement, 'every scribe who has been trained for the kingdom of heaven is like the master of a household who brings out of his treasures what is new and what is old', reflects Matthew's view of himself as something of a Christian sage.

In his Infancy Narrative, Matthew firmly asserted that Jesus is son of David and son of Abraham: Saviour of Jew and Gentile. At the same time, his ancestry shows him to be wholly one of us, 'like his brothers and sisters in every respect' (Heb 2:17). Virginally conceived, Jesus is God-with-us. Son of David, he was, appropriately, born in Bethlehem. The Gentile Magi acknowledged the king of the Jews. He re-enacted the Exodus of his people and, figuratively, suffered their Exile. As 'the Nazarene' he embarked on his mission. The Sermons follow the stages of the mission.

In the Sermon on the Mount (Chapters 5-7) Jesus addressed his people; the beatitudes are thoroughly Jewish in form and content. He assured his people that he had not come to abolish *Torah* and Prophets; he was their prophetic fulfilment. His challenge broadened and deepened the meaning of the term 'righteousness', the doing of God's will. For the Christian, the ultimate authority is not the Law of Moses but 'these words of mine'.

Jesus was sent 'only to the lost sheep of the house of Israel'. The initial mission of the Twelve had the same limitation. Matthew's community saw itself as the authentic way of Judaism. Mission brings trial. They must maintain trust in God. They, and those who hearkened to them, will be compensated by a generous God. Jesus spoke in parables. His purposes were unequivocal: to challenge and teach. Matthew, in the Sermon in Parables (Chapter 13), gives the impression that Jesus was reacting to the rejection of his word; his parables were a punishment of unfaith. Again, the evangelist displays his preoccupation: the struggle with contemporary Judaism.

A Christian community needs structure, but there is inherent danger. This is brought out in the Sermon on the Church (Chapter 18). It is the special duty of leaders to care for the weak and the vulnerable and not, through insensitivity, to make their lot harder. All members of a community should display mutual concern, especially where there is need of correction. Forgiveness – 'seventy times seven' – is the hallmark; they are to mirror the conduct of an infinitely forgiving *Abba*. As for the exercise of authority, Chapter 23 shows, eloquently, how authority is *not* to be exercised. Jesus had stood authority on its head: *exousia* (authority) is shown in *diakonia* (service). Already, by Matthew's day, Christian leaders were sporting titles and flexing ecclesiastical muscle.

The Judgment Sermon (Chs 24-25) uses the prospect of eschatological trials to exhort Christians to respond to present difficulties. Parables figure prominently. The Parable of *The Talents* challenges an image of God as exacting taskmaster: it inhibits. The image of a generous God is liberating: one will dare to risk. The Last Judgment serves as an imperative call to action in the here-and-now. Jesus' solidarity with all who suffer copper-fastens his image of the gracious God who shows a preferential option for the poor. In his Passion (Chs 26-27), Jesus, abandoned by his followers, faced the hour of trial alone. In Gethsemane he suffered the challenge of painful choice; on Calvary the anguish of Godforsakenness. All the evangelists stress the innocence of Jesus and have Pilate witness to it. Matthew underlines the fact by presenting the death of Jesus as the heinous crime of the shedding of innocent blood. This is acknowledged by Judas and the priests and, dramatically, by Pilate in his futile washing of hands. The Magi had come to seek 'the king of the Jews'; Jesus died as King of the Jews. The further significance of his death was marked, symbolically, by apocalyptic signs. The centurion and his men confessed, in awe: 'Truly this man was God's Son!'

Death was not the end. The women, who had come to mourn a dead Jesus, were met by the risen Lord. He gave them a message for his 'brothers' – their failure is forgiven: they will see him in Galilee. And when they met they received the commission: 'Go therefore and make disciples of all nations'. As well as the assurance: 'And remember, I am with you always, to the end of the age'.

LUKE: THE QUALITY OF MERCY

Luke, author of the Third Gospel and Acts of the Apostles, was a second- or, perhaps, third-generation Christian. He was, seemingly, a Gentile and a native, very likely, of Syrian Antioch. He was well educated, a fact borne out by the quality and flexibility of his Greek. He was, evidently, well versed in the Greek Bible. It is not possible to determine where Luke-Acts was written. As to date of authorship, it was written after Mark (usually dated around 70 CE). The Gospel presupposes the destruction of Jerusalem by the Romans (Lk 13:35; 21:20). The prevailing tendency is to date the whole work to 80-85 CE.

It is unfortunate that an understandable desire to group the four gospels meant the separation of Acts of the Apostles from the Gospel of Luke. The fact is, Gospel and Acts belong together as two parts of a single work. The Gospel begins in Jerusalem, more specifically in the Temple, with the message of the angel to Zechariah; it closes with the disciples of Jesus at prayer in the Temple (Lk 24:53). The plan of Acts is firmly sketched in Acts 1:18 – 'You will be my witnesses in Jerusalem, in all Judaea and Samaria, and to the ends of the earth'. Jerusalem is central. In the Gospel, the movement is *toward* Jerusalem; in Acts the movement is *away from* Jerusalem. For Luke, the city and its temple are symbols of the people of Israel.

When Gospel and Acts, together, are taken into account, one can appreciate Luke's purpose and achievement. Then one can see that his object was to present the definitive stage of God's saving plan from the birth of the Baptist to the proclamation of the Good News in the capital of the Gentile world – Rome. Luke has traced a continuous line from the Scriptures of Israel into the birth, life, death and resurrection of Jesus, and from Jesus into the community of Jesus' followers. Thus, the Christian community has continuity with Israel and identity with God's purpose.

CHRISTOLOGY

Luke is a theologian of salvation history – the entrance of salvation into history. He alludes to a basic divine 'plan' for the salvation of humankind, one that was being realised in the activity of Jesus (7:30). The concept of such a plan is what underlines the 'necessity' – *e.g.* 'was it not necessary that the Messiah should suffer these things and then enter into his glory?' (24:26) – which is often associated with what Jesus does or says and with what happens as fulfilment of Scripture. That the plan of God concerns the 'salvation' of humankind receives special emphasis in the Lucan writings.

Luke has told the Jesus-story not only with christological but with soteriological intent: what Jesus did, said and suffered had and has a significance for, and a bearing on, human history. Acts 4:12 makes this clear: 'there is salvation in no one else, for there is no other name under heaven given among mortals by which we must be saved'. Then there is the manner in which Luke regards the effects of the Christ-event. While the verbal form 'to forgive sins' is frequent in the Synoptics, the abstract form 'forgiveness of sins' is a Lucan usage. Luke sums up Jesus' work as the release of men and women from their debts (sins) in the sight of God. By all that he was and all that he did, he has cancelled the debt incurred by their sinful conduct. In the sayings of Jesus, 'peace' stands for the bounty he brings to humankind. And if he seems to deny that his coming brings peace (12:51), it is because he knows that men and women will have to make a decision about him, either for him or against him. Those who accept him into their lives will know the peace which he alone can bring.

VINDICATOR OF THE POOR

Jesus knew it to be his vocation to proclaim the true God – the Father. He knew that in faithfulness to his task he was making the kingdom present. How he saw his task is vividly portrayed in Luke's introduction of Jesus' ministry in 4:16-21. In his programmatic statement the Lucan Jesus pointed to the recipients of his good news: captives, blind, oppressed – all who are weakest and powerless. They are 'the poor'. There are also the rich. Luke, paradoxically, is evangelist of the rich and respected. That is to say, he wants to motivate them towards conversion in keeping with the social message of Jesus.

Luke had, evidently, to face the problem of wealth in his own community. If there were no absolutely needy members, there were those relatively well off. These were, by and large, the 'Pharisees': significantly, Luke characterised Pharisees as 'lovers of money' (16:14). He was perceptively aware of two attitudes fostered by riches: a false sense of security and a lack of appreciation of and concern for the plight of the poor. Indeed, he was conscious that Mammon might become one's god (16:13). He also had to inculcate the practice of almsgiving among people (Gentile Christians) for whom almsgiving was not part of their culture (as it was for Jewish Christians). Luke, besides, had two aspects of ancient Mediterranean life in mind. To share with someone without expectation of return was, on the one hand, tantamount to treating them as kin, as family. On the other hand, to refuse to share was tantamount to regarding them as being outside one's community. In this context, giving to the poor meant friendship with the poor, communion with them. The other factor was the patron-client relationship – a situation in which the client was ever in debt to the patron. The giving without expectation of return urged by the Lucan Jesus was a blow to this relationship. For that matter, Luke was convinced that relief of human need and suffering was the one and only positive contribution of money – 'you must give up all that you have'. There is yet another dimension. Luke, throughout Luke-Acts, consistently uses authority over material possessions as a symbol for spiritual authority.

FRIEND OF SINNERS

Jesus was not primarily a preacher of repentance; he proclaimed the imminent coming of the kingdom as salvation. The parables of God seeking the lost (Lk 15:3-6, 8-9), once Luke's conclusions (15:7,10) are removed, can be seen as focused, not on repentance, but on God's initiative and action. The one distinctive note that we can be certain marked Jesus' teaching about the kingdom is that it would include the 'sinners'. There should be no confusion about the basic meaning of the term 'sinners' in the gospels. It comes from the Hebrew *reshaim* – the wicked, the non-observant who were reckoned to have placed themselves outside the covenant. Jesus saw his mission as being in a special manner to the 'lost' and the 'sinners'. He was also concerned with the poor, the meek, the downtrodden. If there was conflict, it was about the status of the 'wicked'. 'This fellow welcomes sinners and even eats with them!' He counted such within his fellowship. This was conduct that genuinely caused serious offence.

Luke has a gentle soul. Because of this he has discerned the tenderness of Jesus. He has assembled the three parables of Chapter 15: the Lost Sheep, the Lost Coin, the Lost Boy (Prodigal Son). In all three, God rejoices over the homecoming of the lost. We, too, must have something of the mercy of a forgiving God. The father's gentle rebuke to the sulking elder son has a message for all of us: 'we had to celebrate and rejoice, because this brother of yours was dead and has come to life; he was lost and has been found' (15:32).

Perhaps nowhere more than in the moving passage on the 'woman of the city who was a sinner' (7:36-50) do we see Jesus as Luke saw him. The Lord does not hesitate between the self-righteous one and the sinner, and his words are clear and to the point: 'therefore, I tell you, her sins, which were many, have been forgiven; hence she has shown great love' (7:47). Luke also records the words of Jesus to the 'good thief' (23:43) and his prayer for those who engineered his death: 'Father, forgive them; for they do not know what they are doing' (23:34). Everywhere, at all times, there is forgiveness. It has been well said that the Gospel of Luke is the Gospel of great pardons.

DEATH AND VINDICATION

While Luke's passion narrative is based on Mark's version, it differs from Mark in structure and tone. Luke has some affinity with the Johannine tradition. Indeed, one might say that Luke's portrait of Jesus is halfway between the passion pictures of Mark and of John. His Jesus is not the anguished man of Mark's Gethsemane and cross. Nor is he yet the majestic Jesus who dominates the Johannine story. Luke's Jesus, though rejected and mocked and suffering, is ever in serene communion with the Father. He does not experience Godforsakenness. His death is not with a lonely cry but with tranquil prayer, 'Father, into your hands I commend my spirit' (Lk 23:46).

Perhaps the most distinctive, surely the most comforting, theme of Luke's passion narrative is his depiction of the healing and forgiving power of God flowing from Jesus throughout the passion. Jesus healed the wound of one of those who came to arrest him. He healed the enmity that had existed between his judges (Pilate and Herod). He looked upon a fallen Peter with deep compassion.

He prayed forgiveness on those who had brought about his death, acknowledging that they did not really know what they had done. He promised to take with him into the presence of his Father a wrongdoer who simply asked to be remembered by him. In all of this Jesus is manifestly the Jesus who 'walks' through the pages of Luke. But never more clearly than in the passion narrative is Luke – in Dante's phrase, *scriba mansuetudinis Cristi*[2] – the chronicler of Christ's gentleness of character. We need Mark's story to remind us of the awfulness of the deed and to urge us to come to terms with the reality of the cross. And we need Luke's gentler story to discern the forgiving love of God shining through the worst that humankind can wreak.

SUGGESTIONS FOR FURTHER READING

General

P.J.Achtemeier, J.B.Green, M.M.Thompson, *Introducing the New Testament*. Its Literature and Theology (Grand Rapids/Cambridge: Eerdmans, 2001).

R.E.Brown, *An Introduction to the New Testament* (New York/London: Doubleday, 1997).

G. Stanton, *The Gospels and Jesus* [2nd ed.] (Oxford: OUP,2002).

J.P.Meier, *A Marginal Jew*. 3 vols, (New York: Doubleday, 1991,1994, 2001).

Mark

J.R.Donahue, D.J. Harrington, *The Gospel of Mark* (Collegeville, MN: The Liturgical Press, 2002).

W.J.Harrington, *Mark: Realistic Theologian* (Dublin: The Columba Press, 1996).

F.J.Moloney, *The Gospel of Mark*. A Commentary (Peabody,MA: Hendrickson, 2002).

W.R. Telford, *The Theology of the Gospel of Mark* (Cambridge: CUP, 1999).

2. Dante Alighieri, *Monarchia*, I, 16, 2.

Matthew

D.J. Harrington, *The Gospel of Matthew* (Collegeville, MN: The Liturgical Press, 1991).

W.J.Harrington, *Matthew: Sage Theologian* (Dublin: The Columba Press, 1998).

J.D. Kingsbury, *Matthew As Story* (Philadelphia: Fortress, 1988).

J.P.Meier, *Matthew* (Wilmington, DE: M. Glazier, 1980).

Luke

F.W. Danker, *Jesus and the New Age. A Commentary on St Luke's Gospel* (Philadelphjia: Fortress, 1988).

J.A. Fitzmyer, *The Gospel According to Luke.* 2 vols (New York: Doubleday, 1981, 1985).

W.J. Harrington, *Luke: Gracious Theologian* (Dublin: The Columba Press, 1997).

L.T.Johnson, *Luke* (Collegeville, MN: The Liturgical Press, 1993)

III

A Note on Gospel Sources:

questions about *Q* and the fresh emergence
of Proto-Luke: a recent shift in the quest for
a missing link behind the Gospels

THOMAS L. BRODIE, OP

A NOTE ON GOSPEL SOURCES[1]

Thomas L. Brodie, OP

The relationship between the gospels has always been a puzzle. They are obviously linked, but it has been difficult to say how. Part of the answer has slowly become clear. After decades of patient examination it is now generally agreed that Matthew and Luke both used Mark. Oral tradition does not explain the links; the similarities are such that they require a connection that is written. Matthew and Luke both had copies of Mark's text. However, once that has been established, the picture blurs. Making further connections is not easy. Yet there is the hope that further decades of patient work will eventually unscramble the puzzle. The matter is important because it casts light on the way the New Testament writings were composed and on the way God's self-revelation comes to us – ultimately on the way God is present in our lives.

One thing is generally agreed. While Matthew and Luke both shared Mark they also shared something else. For instance, in their early chapters both Matthew and Luke report something that is missing in Mark: a long sermon by Jesus, the Sermon on the Mount (Matthew 5-7) and the Sermon on the Plain (Luke 6:12-49). Both sermons contain beatitudes, and both are followed almost immediately by the account of the healing of the centurion's servant.

Again, oral tradition, despite its initial plausibility, does not explain the similarity. Matthew and Luke have so much in common that apart from using Mark's written text, they also have some other written connection, or they shared some other source. But what was it? There are two main possibilities.

A LOST SOURCE (Q)

One solution, first formulated clearly in 1890, is quite simply that Matthew and Mark both shared a source that, unlike Mark,

---

1. The detailed arguments for this brief contribution are given in the author's *The Birthing of the New Testament. The Intertextual Development of the New Testament Writings*, Sheffield: Sheffield Phoenix Press, 2004.

has now been lost. We do not know its content, except by looking at the non-Marcan material shared by Matthew and Luke. And we do not know its name, so it is simply called the Source or more often Q, from *Quelle*, German for source.

The idea that Q ever existed has had a chequered career. In one sense it has been highly successful, and has often appeared rock solid. It has two powerful factors in its favour. It fills a gap; and it does so with a minimum of effort. Suddenly, the origin of the gospels seems to become much clearer: Matthew and Luke had two main sources, Mark and Q. The diagram of the Two Source Theory has become very common, especially in textbooks. People have even begun to speak of the Q community.

In recent years the idea of Q has received a fresh boost. It has come into the open, so to speak. Formerly it often seemed vague; it was not clear what did or did not belong to it. When Matthew and Luke give different accounts of the healing of the centurion's servant, for instance, which of them is reflecting Q, and which is introducing changes? Or have both of them changed Q? And if so, how do we know what Q really looked like?

However, that phase of research has moved on. A major team of scholars undertook a project, the International Q Project, organised mostly from Claremont, California and Bamberg, Germany, but with help from Leuven, Belgium. This team has spent years sifting the shared details generally attributed to Q, and has attempted to reconstruct the original Q.

The process of reconstruction was often brutally taxing. Apart from working in their home cities or towns, the researchers would gather together from time to time, especially in the days before biblical conferences, and plough ever so slowly through tiny details ('Does this *kai* [and], found in Matthew but missing in Luke, really belong to Q'?) Having sat as an observer through several days of this process, year after year, I was constantly torn between disbelief and admiration. Particular credit goes to one of the leaders, James Robinson. He was incredibly patient. For hour after hour he stayed with the detail of the discussions and with the slow process of voting: the discussions were concluded by voting. Yet he could also stand back and laugh, and even laugh gently at the hazardousness of what the research team was attempting. Eventually, in 2000, the team published their conclusions[2]. The result for Q, however, is ambiguous. The new clarity concerning the hypothesis provides an improved opportunity for judging whether it should be retained or replaced. In a curious way the theory's former vagueness helped it. It was hard to argue against it, because it was not clear what it was. Now that it is in the open, so to speak, it has become more vulnerable.

The vulnerability of the Q theory has been highlighted by, for instance, two Birmingham scholars, Michael Goulder and Mark Goodacre. One argument is that the Q theory is simply unnecessary. Rather than postulate an unknown source, why not simply say that Luke, as well as using Mark, also copied from Matthew, but adapted it? This would explain the similarities between Luke and Matthew.

But could Luke do such a thing? Just how much adaptation could Luke introduce? What kind was Luke? What is otherwise known of Luke and his way of using sources?

LUKE AND THE ANCIENT WAY OF USING SOURCES

It is generally agreed that Luke was a writer in the Greco-Roman ('Hellenistic') mode, and it is also becoming widely recognised that Greco-Roman writers adapted existing texts with a complex mix of imitation and inventiveness (*imitatio* and *emulatio*).

It is also generally agreed that, apart from using Mark, Luke made massive use of a Greek translation of the Old Testament, specifically the Septuagint version, and that he adapted it in all sorts of ways. He used it to formulate his text so that his account of Jesus gave new expression to the Old Testament. Thus, his way of adapting the Septuagint contributed to the vast phenomenon whereby the Old Testament is fulfilled in the New.

As one examines Luke's use of the Septuagint a striking phenomenon emerges. Within the fifty-two chapters of Luke-Acts lies a stream of passages, a total of about 25 chapters, that stands apart. Three reasons indicate this standing apart.

2. James M. Robinson, Paul Hoffmann and John S. Kloppenborg, edd., *The Critical Edition of Q*, Hermeneia; Minneapolis: Fortress, and Leuven: Peeters, 2000.

1. These passages have a distinctive dependence on the Septuagint, a dependence that is indicated by a wide range of verifiable connections. (These passages use other sources also, including specifically Christian ones).

2. The passages form a specific unity, coherent and complete, with a clear structure that is modelled precisely on one of the great prophetic histories of the Old Testament, the Elijah-Elisha narrative (1 Kings 16:29 – 2 Kings 13).

3. When this specific unity is seen on its own, it explains other New Testament data, especially about the gospels.

The stream of passages may be summarised under the following headings:

Jesus' infancy narrative: Luke 1-2

Jesus' early ministry: Luke 3:1-4:22a (except 3:7-9; 4:1-13); 7:1-8:3

Jesus' journey to Jerusalem: Luke 9:51-10:20; 16:1-9,19-31; 17:11-18:8; 19:1-10

Jesus' death and resurrection: Luke 22-24 (except 22:31-65)

The church's beginnings: Acts 1:1-2:42

The church's early ministry: Acts 2:43-5:42

The church's move away from Jerusalem: Acts 6:1-9:30

The church's transformation, integrating the Gentiles: Acts 9:31-15:35.

The simplest, best explanation for this Old Testament-related phenomenon is that it is the long-sought first version of Luke-Acts, what some scholars call Proto-Luke[3].

Once Proto-Luke is in place, it becomes relatively easy to understand the sequence of the Gospels and Acts. Proto-Luke was first, and was used – as one of many sources – by Mark. Mark in turn was adapted, along with Proto-Luke and other sources, by Matthew. Then John used Matthew (and other sources). Finally,

---

3. In 1891 Paul Feine of Göttingen established a central hypothesis: Luke-Acts once existed in a shorter form, a form that was independent of the gospel of Mark. The subsequent history of the idea went through many phases and in some forms became known as Proto-Luke.

canonical Luke-Acts used John and the earlier texts, including Proto-Luke, Mark *and Matthew*. This final step, because it includes Luke's adaptation of Matthew, explains the (non-Marcan) similarities between Matthew and Luke.

In outline, therefore, the sequence of the gospels emerges as follows:

Proto-Luke
Mark
Matthew
John
Luke-Acts

This is the literary backbone. The full pattern of dependence is far more complex, with influences from other writings and from the intense social and historical events of the first century.

PROTO-LUKE AND Q: ASPECTS OF COMPARISON

In a comparison between Proto-Luke and Q, it may seem at first that Q has the advantage. Q is immediately attractive. Details apart, it seems to solve problems with a minimum of effort. Proto-Luke needs more work and patience. Yet, in the final analysis the Proto-Luke hypothesis is more solid, for the following reasons:

1. *The logic of the general argument.* At first it can appear that the claims of both hypotheses – Proto-Luke and Q – are equal. Each uses the similarity between two fixed texts to invoke a third. The similarity between Matthew and Luke is used to invoke Q. The similarity between Luke-Acts and the Septuagint is used to invoke Proto-Luke. However, Q strains logic in a way that Proto-Luke does not. Proto-Luke is stable, and is fully present in Luke-Acts. In other words, Luke-Acts contains it in its entirety, and unchanged. Q, however, is not fully contained either in Matthew or Luke, and so the reconstruction of its wording is extremely hazardous. It is therefore out of sight, hidden in a way that Proto-Luke is not. It asks for forms of verses that have never been seen. This in itself does not discount Q, but it asks logic to go further, to claim more; and so, in comparison to Proto-Luke, it is weaker.

2. *The logic of specific verses.* If a verse from Luke-Acts can be rooted either in the Septuagint or Q, priority goes to the Septuagint.

Other things being equal, it is more logical, more credible, to attribute a text to a source that is certain (the Septuagint) than to a text that is hypothetical (Q). Again, therefore, in evenly balanced disputes about the parentage of verses, the Septuagint has the edge.

3. *General background.* Proto-Luke has a specific verifiable model (the Elijah-Elisha narrative) where Q does not. (The role of the gospel of Thomas as a model for Q is problematic. It is not certain that Thomas or a Thomas-like text predated Q. Furthermore, the genre of Thomas does not fit Q well. Thomas is simple, all sayings where Q is more complex, combining sayings with narrative.)

4. *Structure.* Proto-Luke has a precise verifiable structure; Q does not.

5. *Effectiveness.* In the long term, Proto-Luke works better. It accounts for almost all Q texts, either directly, or indirectly (through its influence on Matthew and canonical Luke), or in conjunction with a further verifiable dependence (that of some Matthean sayings on Deuteronomy). Also, it accounts for far more gospel data, beginning with Mark's Gospel. In other words, it solves more problems than Q and does so more comprehensively.

It seems reasonable then, at the very least, to give Proto-Luke equal time.

IV

Jesus and Paul: Child Refugees

JEROME MURPHY-O'CONNOR, OP

JESUS AND PAUL: CHILD REFUGEES

Jerome Murphy-O'Connor, OP

An extraordinary series of coincidences links the lives of Jesus and Paul, *e.g.* both were born in the two or three years preceding the death of Herod the Great in 4 BC; both were killed by the Roman authorities; and there are many others. These I plan to study in detail in a book provisionally entitled *Jesus and Paul. Parallel Lives.* The coincidence that I want to highlight here is the fact that both became refugees while still children. Too young to understand, they undoubtedly felt, however obscurely, the fear emanating from their parents as they faced a future of danger and uncertainty, far from the security of the familiar.

JESUS

One of the two sources that enabled Matthew to write Ch. 2 of his Gospel is the story of the flight of Joseph and his family into Egypt and eventual return to Palestine[1]. It reads:

> (13) Behold, an angel of the Lord appeared to Joseph in a dream, and said, 'Rise, take the child and his mother, and flee to Egypt, and remain there till I tell you, for Herod is about to search, to destroy him.' (14) And he arose and took the child and his mother by night, and departed to Egypt, (15) and remained there until the death of Herod [when] (19) behold an angel appeared in a dream to Joseph saying, (20) 'Rise take the child and his mother, and go to the land of Israel, for those who sought the child's life are dead.' (21). And he rose and took the child and his mother and went into the land of Israel (Mt 2:13-21).

This simple story contains no problems, but it does give rise to a question that is not often asked. Why was such an event ever remembered? Not only does it have no relationship to the ministry of Jesus, but he is too young to be an active agent. He does nothing. He is simply there as a mere appendage of his parents. It is they

1. For the justification of this statement see my 'The Childhood of Jesus: Matthew's Version', *Biblical Review* (forthcoming)

who are the actors in the story. Jesus' place is so far in the background that one is forced to wonder why the story was ever told about him.

There was one group in the early church, however, who had a vital interest in the story, namely, Jewish Christians. With great insight David Daube wrote,

> Imagine the Jews who adhered to Jesus celebrating the Passover in the years following the crucifixion. We know that they went on celebrating it fully since the Temple was not yet destroyed. As such a group – a family outside Jerusalem, a band of pilgrims in the city – assembled in the evening to dwell on the rescue from Egypt, the pattern of divine intervention and salvation, is it conceivable that they confined themselves to the customary tales, reflections and prayers, without introducing what was for them the fulfilment of it all? Surely not.[2]

The story of Jesus in Egypt offered Jewish Christians a supplemental way to Christianise Passover. Even though he was too young to have had any responsibility, Jesus had lived through a traumatic event that paralleled the experience of the Jewish people as symbolised by Jacob in the *Passover Haggadah* (to which the numbers in the following paragraph refer)[3].

The points of contact between the two narratives are striking. Jacob is threatened by Laban (I, 1), as Jesus was by Herod, but the move to Egypt is directly motivated by a divine command (II, 1), which in the Flight-Return story is mediated by an angel[4]. In both cases the sojourn in Egypt is intended to be temporary (II, 2), *i.e.* until the danger ceased. Equally the return from Egypt is the work of the Lord (VII, 1). Moreover, Laban is identified as an Aramean,

---

2. David Daube, 'The Earliest Structure of the Gospels', *New Testament Studies* 5 (1958-59) 174-75

3. The dating is discussed and the complete text given in L. Finkelstein, 'The Oldest Midrash: Pre-Rabbinic Ideals and Teaching in the Passover Haggadah', *Harvard Theological Review* 31 (1938) 291-317

4. Like a number of late texts, the *Passover Haggadah* saw angels as a danger to monotheism, for example the comment on 'And the Lord brought us forth from Egypt' is 'Not by means of an angel, nor by means of a messenger, but the Holy One, blessed be He, Himself' (VII, 1)

whereas Herod was an Idumean. In the square Aramaic consonantal script the difference is only one letter, *'rmy* 'Aramean' versus *'dmy* 'Idumean'. The shape of the two letters is almost the same, which facilitated a punning reference. They each have horizontal and vertical elements, but in *daleth* the junction is right-angled, whereas in *resh* it is curved. It is a further point of similarity that both Laban 'who sought to destroy the whole family' (I, 1) and Herod were hated half-Jews. Finally, both texts evoke the execution of children (VI, 2).

Since it was the *Passover Haggadah* (among other material) that determined why Jesus' childhood sojourn in Egypt was retained in the popular memory, it was inevitable that this text should influence the way that the story of this episode was told, particularly the emphasis on the providential dimension. Such literary colouring has given rise in some quarters to the belief that the *Passover Haggadah* inspired the creation of the Flight-Return story, which is why some scholars believe that it never really happened. Were this the case, however, Jesus would certainly have been presented as an adult in order to wear the haggadic mantle of Jacob. The hypothesis of pure creativity cannot explain why Jesus is depicted as *a child*. A fact of his childhood stands at the beginning of the development process[5], and it is this that we must now question.

It is extremely doubtful that Herod the Great had the slightest interest in the child Jesus. A child could neither plot nor threaten, and Herod knew that he himself was close to death. It is inconceivable that he would want to exterminate someone who just might be a potential enemy a generation into the future. Herod was concerned with imminent danger, and in this respect Bethlehem certainly worried him deeply.

Herod had to contend with enemies throughout his life. Josephus tells us that, for his protection,

---

5. The burden of proof lies on those who claim that New Testament writers used Jewish texts to create Jesus-narratives out of whole cloth. Not only is it intrinsically more probable that a fact stimulated recollection of an older text, but it can also be demonstrated, for example, that Matthew was stimulated to think of Zechariah 9:9 because of Mark's story of the entry into Jerusalem (11:1-7), which Matthew then rewrote to make the prophecy the centre point of his narrative (21:1-7). Similarly in the *Pesharim* from Qumran it is clear that the Essenes read their history *into* the biblical texts and not the other way around.

There were spies set everywhere both in the city and on the roads who watched those who met together; it is even reported that he did not neglect this part of caution, but that he would sometimes disguise himself as a private individual and mix among the multitude in the night time in order to test what opinion they had of his rule" (Josephus, *Antiquities of the Jews* 15.366-67).

In 7 BC Herod had his sons Alexander and Aristobulus executed on suspicion of treason. In 5 BC Herod learnt that another son, Antipater, had conspired to poison him. Late that year when Herod became ill, there was a tentative uprising in Jerusalem. Herod burnt the ringleaders alive, and had the others executed also (Josephus, *Jewish War* 1.647-55).

Under these conditions it would be extraordinary if Herod had not taken very seriously the prophecy of a warrior king who would come from Bethlehem,

But you, O Bethlehem of Ephrathah,
who are one of the little clans of Judah,
from you shall come forth for me
one who is to rule in Israel (Micah 5:1).

From Herod's perspective this was incitement to rebellion. An opponent could recruit forces much more easily if he claimed to be the promised Messiah from Bethlehem. As God's Chosen One he was guaranteed success; he could not lose. It would be extremely naive to imagine that Herod's secret police were not all over Bethlehem just waiting for someone to step out of line.

Since Herod was prepared to execute his own sons on mere suspicion, one did not have to be a genius to realise that he would have no compunction about wiping out a whole village just to give himself peace of mind. In point of fact, in 37 BC, at the beginning of his reign, Herod had all the members of the Sanhedrin executed, because it had once dared to charge him with murder when he was governor of Galilee (Josephus, *Antiquities of the Jews* 14.175).

Given what everyone knew about Herod's character and temperament, it would be incredible if those who were free to leave Bethlehem and seek safety outside Herod's jurisdiction did not avail of the opportunity. Egypt was the traditional place of refuge for those in danger in Judea (1 Kgs 11:40; 2 Kgs 25:25-26; Jer 26:20-21), and it was not very far away. By the ancient roads it was a week's walk (170 kms) from Bethlehem to the Wadi el-Arish, 'the River of Egypt'(1 Kgs 8:65; Judith 1:9), the traditional border between Egypt and Judah. Once across that border the fugitives would have been in a Roman province, on whose territory Herod would not dare to intrude.

Joseph's skill as an artisan gave him mobility. He could find work anywhere. He was not tied to land as were the farmers and shepherds. There can be no doubt about the historicity of the flight into Egypt of Jesus and his family. In fact, I would be extremely surprised if they were the only ones to flee from Bethlehem.

We have no way of knowing where the Holy Family settled in Egypt, or how long they had to stay there before Herod died. The Flight-Return source informed Matthew that the Holy Family did return to the land of Israel on getting news of the death of the king. At that point Matthew was able to supplement his source by what had become common knowledge. Joseph and his family did not return to Bethlehem, but instead took up residence in Nazareth, far to the north in Galilee (Mt 2:22-23).

There are two issues here. Why did Joseph avoid Bethlehem where he had a house (Mt 2:11) and friends? And why did he opt for Nazareth as an alternative?

Matthew answers the first question, 'when Joseph heard that Archelaus reigned over Judea in place of his father Herod, he was afraid to go there' (2:22). It is possible that Matthew had specific information regarding Joseph's motivation. But if he did not, his explanation is eminently plausible.

Even before he went to Rome to claim his inheritance, Archelaus slew 3,000 of those who opposed him (Josephus, *Jewish War* 2.1-13). His reputation was so bad that a Jewish delegation was sent to Rome from Jerusalem to beg the emperor Augustus not to approve his nomination as king (Josephus, *Jewish War* 2.80-92). Augustus, however, went ahead as regards the land willed to Archelaus, but denied him the royal title (Josephus, *Jewish War* 2.93). While all this infighting was going on in Rome, the Roman general P. Quinctilius Varus, the Roman governor of Syria, had to stamp out a rebellion in Palestine. At the end of his campaign he crucified 2,000 people

(Josephus, *Jewish War* 2.66-79). Even the most politically unaware could see that it was not the time to return to Judea, particularly since the expected consequences of Archelaus' disappointment were fully realised when he returned home. 'He used not only the Jews, but the Samaritans also, barbarously, and this out of resentment at their old quarrels with him' (Josephus, *Jewish War* 2.111). Clearly the inhabitants of Bethlehem would have been in even greater danger than in the days of Herod the Great. Archelaus had to face more overt opposition than his father and so had good reason to fear the appearance of a warlike Messiah from Bethlehem.

Matthew gives us no answer to the second question, but it is highly probable that Joseph's choice of Nazareth was motivated by economic considerations.

Herod's will gave Galilee to another son, Antipas. He, however, inherited a kingdom without a capital. In putting down the rebellion that followed Herod's death in 4 BC Varus burnt Sepphoris to the ground (Josephus, *Jewish War* 2.68). Antipas' first concern was to rebuild Sepphoris bigger and more beautiful in emulation of his father, who had built new cities at Caesarea, Antipatris, and Phasaelis, in addition to rebuilding Sebaste and Agrippias[6]. The original size of Sepphoris is unknown, but it is estimated that Antipas planned for a population of 25,000.[7]

Once word went out that Antipas was recruiting a labour force, Joseph realised that he would have work on the site for 10-12 years, the average period for the building of a Herodian city (Josephus, *Antiquities of the Jews* 15.341; 16.136). But it would be unwise to put his wife and children in the rough conditions of a great international work camp. Nazareth, only four kilometres away, was clearly visible to the west across the valley. There his family could live undisturbed at the price of an hour's walk to work. And he could develop a second business there, to which his sons (Mk 6:3) could contribute.

Villages, however, are notoriously unreceptive to newcomers. There would have been no overt hostility, but neither would there have been the warm welcome that would make the refugees from

---

6. Peter Richardson, *Herod. King of the Jews and Friend of the Romans* (Columbia: University of South Carolina Press, 1996) 177

7. Harold Hoehner, *Herod Antipas* (Grand Rapids: Zonervan, 1972) 52

Bethlehem feel at home. For a year, perhaps longer, they would have been regarded with suspicion. Was Joseph an agent of the new king? Might he be reporting to the tax collectors? Patiently he and his family had to win their place in a new society, while Jesus' interest in, and curiosity about, the very different world of Sepphoris increased as he grew.

PAUL

It is an extraordinary coincidence that the circumstances that brought Jesus to Galilee were precisely those that forced Paul and his family out of Galilee into exile.

It is a further coincidence that Luke made the same mistake regarding the origins of Jesus and Paul. Jesus was known as Jesus of Nazareth. Hence, Luke assumed that his parents were natives of Nazareth, and that his birth in Bethlehem was an accident. Matthew tells a more accurate story[8]. Similarly Paul was known as Paul of Tarsus, and Luke in consequence assumed that he had been born there (Acts 22:3), but it is more probable that he acquired the name simply because he grew up there, just as Jesus got his name because he grew up in Nazareth.

If Matthew's version of the origins of Jesus contradicts that of Luke, so the latter's account of the origins of Paul, is contradicted by Jerome of Bethlehem. In 387 or 388 he wrote a commentary on Paul's letter to Philemon in which he said apropos of vv. 23-24,

> We have heard this story. They say that the parents of the Apostle Paul were from Gischala, a region of Judea, and that, when the whole province was devastated by the hand of Rome and the Jews scattered throughout the world, they were moved to Tarsus, a town of Cilicia; the boy Paul inherited the lot of his parents. Thus we can understand what he says of himself 'Are they Hebrews? So am I. Are they Israelites? So am I. Are the seed of Abraham? So am I' (2 Cor 11:22), and also elsewhere 'A Hebrew born of Hebrews' (Phil 3:5), and other things which suggest that he was much more a Judean than a Tarsian (*Patrologia Latina* 26.617).

8. The census that is the lynchpin of Lk 1-2 cannot be historical (Schürer, *History*, 1.399-427). Thus the only framework for the childhood of Jesus is that of Mt 1-2, according to which Mary and Joseph were natives of Bethlehem.

Four or five years later Jerome wrote a biographical dictionary of one hundred and thirty-five Christian authors entitled *Famous Men*. Naturally Paul figured prominently; his biography is the fifth and opens with the words,

> Paul, an apostle, previously called Saul, was not one of the Twelve Apostles. He was of the tribe of Benjamin and of the town of Gischala in Judea. When the town was captured by the Romans he migrated with his parents to Tarsus in Cilicia (*Texte und Untersuchungen* 14.9).

The unconditional affirmation that Paul was a Palestinian is found in no other source. In consequence, these two texts must be examined closely. There is only one Gischala in Palestine. Today known as *el-Jish* in Arabic and as *Gush Halav* in modern Hebrew, it is located some five kilometres north of Mount Meiron in Upper Galilee. The name means 'Fat Soil', and Gischala was famous for its olive oil.

The location of Gischala in Galilee should not be understood as a refutation of Jerome's insistence that Gischala was in Judea, because even in the New Testament 'Judea' is used with two distinct meanings. In the narrow sense Judea is distinguished from Galilee and Samaria (Lk 2:4; Acts 9:31). In the wider sense of 'land of the Jews' the term 'englobes' Galilee, *e.g.* 'the word which was proclaimed throughout all Judea beginning from Galilee' (Acts 10:37; cf. Lk 1:5; 23:5). For the Romans from AD 70 onwards the whole area under their control was simply Judea[9], and this is the usage that Jerome and his contemporaries inherited.

The tension between the classification of Gischala as first a 'region' and then a 'town' is more apparent than real. Gischala was in fact a town. But it served as the principal market for the surrounding area, which inevitably took its name from the urban centre. Moreover, Jerome was not particularly interested in geography, and had little personal knowledge of sites in Palestine[10]. Hence, a mistake in his commentary on Philemon is

---

9. Emil Schürer, *The History of the Jewish People in the Age of Jesus Christ (175 BC-AD 135)* (Edinburgh: Clark, 1973) 1.514

10. John Wilkinson, 'L'apport de saint Jérôme à la topographie', *Revue Biblique* 81 (1974) 245-57

understandable. In the interval between this work and *Famous Men*, however, Jerome had translated and updated the *Onomasticum* (a gazetteer of places mentioned in the Bible) of Eusebius of Caesarea which focussed his attention on topography. At the same time Jerome was working on *Hebrew Questions*, in which he drew freely on Josephus, 'the only non-Christian historian he knew thoroughly and whom he had hailed as the Greek Livy'.[11] Gischala appears frequently as a city in the writings of Josephus because it was the home of his detested enemy John ben Levi. Thus, it is not surprising that Gischala should be correctly identified as a town in *Famous Men*.

Where did Jerome get the information about Paul's origins that appears in his commentary on Philemon? In all probability from Origen, whose commentary on Philemon, Jerome's source, unfortunately is no longer extant[12]. Origen must have relied on an oral tradition that he considered trustworthy. I am forced to the same conclusion[13]. Certainly it is impossible to think why anyone should invent Gischala as Paul's birthplace. It is not even mentioned in the Bible. Moreover, Paul identifies himself as a Benjaminite (Phil 3:5), but Gischala is far outside the northern border of the territory of the tribe of Benjamin. Finally, Gischala had no connection with the ministry of Jesus in Galilee, and it had no Christian population in the Byzantine period. In other words, there was nothing to spark invention, and creativity conferred no benefit on anyone.

It is also extremely interesting that Jerome considered 2 Cor 11:22 and Phil 3:5 as *confirmation* of Paul's Palestinian origins. In both of these texts Paul identifies himself both as an 'Israelite'/'of the people of Israel' and a 'Hebrew'. The two terms overlap to a

---

11. J.N.D. Kelly, *Jerome: His Life, Writings, and Controversies* (London: Duckworth, 1975) 153-56

12. Kelly, *Jerome*, 145-49

13. The level of discussion of this point is well illustrated by the brevity of Alfred Plummer's footnote: 'The statement of Jerome that St Paul was born in Gischala in Galilee may safely be disregarded; but his parents may have come from Gischala as emigrants or prisoners of war' (*A Critical and Exegetical Commentary on the Second Epistle of St Paul to the Corinthians* (Edinburgh: Clark, 1915), 320). The one exception is Marco Adinolfi, 'Giscala e S. Paolo', in his *Questioni bibliche di storia e storiografia* (Brescia: Paideia, 1969) 155-164.

considerable extent, and they were used interchangeably at the time of Paul to identify a Jew. It is most unusual, however, to find them used together as here, and the assumption must be that in Paul's mind one added something to the other. 'Israelite' means belonging to Israel, a member of the people of God, and nothing else. 'Hebrew', on the other hand, is often used in the New Testament to mean the language spoken by Jews in Palestine. Luke, for example, depicts Paul speaking to the Jerusalem crowd 'in the Hebrew language' (Acts 21:40; 22:2; 26:14) by which he must have meant Aramaic, which was the spoken language in the first century. The Hebrew text of the Scriptures had to be translated into Aramaic in the synagogue to make it intelligible to the vast majority of Jews who knew no Hebrew[14]. This is confirmed by John, who claimed that the words 'Gabbatha' (19:13; the place where Pilate condemned Jesus) and 'Golgotha' (19:17) were Hebrew, when in fact they were Aramaic[15]. Thus the division between 'Hebrews' and 'Hellenists' among the first Christian converts in Jerusalem was between Aramaic-speakers and those whose language was Greek (Acts 6:1).

In both 2 Cor 11:22 and Phil 3:5, therefore, Paul is proudly claiming to be an Aramaic-speaking Jew who had inherited the language from his parents. As Jerome astutely noted, the immediate inference is that his parents at least had lived in Palestine. Jews in the Greco-Roman world had no need of Aramaic. They used whatever local dialect was necessary for daily living, and learned Greek in order to communicate with a wider world. They did not use the Aramaic targums, but a Greek translation of the Scriptures.

Were Jerome, or Origen for that matter, interested only in explaining how Paul knew Aramaic, the obvious thing to do would have been to appeal to the fact that he was educated in Jerusalem. Paul himself tells us that he had studied Pharisaism there as a young man (Gal 1:14; Phil 3:5). Luke claims that he was a schoolboy there (Acts 22:3; 26:4), which is not in fact correct. That neither Jerome nor Origen made use of such texts strongly suggests that they accepted Gischala as an unavoidable fact to which there were no objections.

14. For the displacement of Hebrew by Aramaic, see Schürer, *History*, 2.20-26

15. Schürer, *History*, 2.22

According to both of Jerome's texts, Paul and his parents were forced out of Gischala by the Romans, who deported them to Tarsus. When did this take place, and why? In terms of what can be determined regarding the date of Paul's birth[16], it is most probable that it was during the disturbances that followed the death of Herod in 4 BC.

The rebellion in Galilee was led by Judas son of Hezekiah, who armed his supporters by breaking into the arsenal of Sepphoris (Josephus, *Antiquities of the Jews* 17.271). In response, the Roman general Varus 'took the city of Sepphoris and burnt it, and made slaves of the inhabitants' (Josephus, *Jewish War* 2.68). The last point does not mean that the citizens became prisoners of war to be liberated once peace had been established. The Roman sold them as slaves and used the money as a contribution to their campaign expenses.

This was standard practice. When Cassius Longinus in his first administration of Syria (53-51 BC) was short of money, 'he made a swift march into Judea, and after taking Tariceae, he carried away 30,000 Jews into slavery' (Josephus, *Jewish War* 1.180). Incidentally this text is significant confirmation of Jerome's usage, because Tariceae (otherwise called Magdala), a city on the Sea of Galilee, is said to be in Judea. During Cassius Longinus' second administration (44-42 BC), when the Jewish inhabitants of Gophna, Emmaus, Lydda, and Thamna failed to pay their taxes, he took the money out of their hides by selling them as slaves (Josephus, *Antiquities of the Jews* 14.275). Hadrian paid for the long and arduous suppression of the Bar Kokhba revolt (132-135 AD) by selling so many slaves that the market was glutted[17].

We must assume, therefore, that the inhabitants of Sepphoris were not the only ones sold into slavery by order of Varus, and that Paul's parents were somehow taken by one of the Roman patrols sent out to collect as many able-bodied individuals as the finance officer of the legion deemed necessary to balance his budget. Women would have been as valuable as men, because slave bred slave. This is not confirmed by what Josephus tells us about the

16. See my *Paul: A Critical Life* (Oxford: Clarendon, 1996) 1-4
17. Schürer, *History*, 1.553

fate of Gischala (*Jewish War* 4.84-120), but he makes it clear that the situation was so confused that Paul's parents could have been picked up virtually anywhere.

Before returning to their base at Antioch-on-the-Orontes (modern Antakya in southern Turkey) the legions would have sold their captives to the omnipresent slave-traders who closely followed every campaign (1 Macc 3:41; 2 Macc 8:11). Philo condemns those 'who, for the sake of lawless gain sell slaves to slave-dealers, and enslave them to any chance persons, transporting them to a foreign land, so that they shall never any more salute their native land, not even in a dream, or taste of any hope of happiness' (*De specialibus legibus* 4.17). For the dealers, however, slaves were just another type of goods. In the Apocalypse merchants lament that 'no one buys their cargo any more, cargo of gold, silver, jewels and pearls, fine linen ... cattle and sheep, horses and chariots, and bodies and human souls' (18:11-13). 'Body' (*sôma*) was a common synonym for 'slave' (*doulos*)[18], and here appears at the bottom of a descending scale of value. Slaves were just a commodity like other animals, to be sold where the demand was greatest.

The baby Paul and his parents were probably shipped out of the nearest port, Ptolemais (modern Akko in northern Israel). As the slave ships worked their way north along the coast, it would not have been good business to have all the ships arrive together at any given port. Prices fell quickly in a saturated market. The slave-dealers must have arranged among themselves to divide or stagger their landfalls.

How many times did Paul's parents experience the degradation of being driven to market, the shame of being offered for sale, before the final humiliation of being handed over to a master? No matter how young Paul was he sensed the emotions of his parents, and was marked for life by the experience. As he grew up and learnt from his Aramaic-speaking parents how they came to be residents of Tarsus, he relived their pain.

Given what Paul went through as the young child of slaves, it is striking that he should have built his vision of reality on two

18. Jennifer Glancy, *Slavery in Early Christianity* (Oxford: Oxford University Press, 2002) 10

extraordinary paradoxes. What the vast majority of those who were free thought of as liberty he insisted was in fact slavery (Gal 4:9; Rom 6:17). Genuine freedom was achieved through a transaction common in the slave-markets. 'You do not belong to yourselves for you were bought with a price' (1 Cor 6:19-20).

CONCLUSION

If I have emphasised the traumatic character of being a childhood refugee, it must not be forgotten that deportation meant that Jesus and Paul grew up in places that gave them advantages which they would never have enjoyed had they stayed in remote country villages such as Bethlehem and Gischala.

Everything that Nazareth had to offer could have been found in Bethlehem with one major exception. Nazareth was within sight and easy reach of Sepphoris, the new capital of Galilee, ruled by a cosmopolitan and Romanophile king. It was in microcosm the complex world of the eastern Mediterranean. Gischala had absolutely nothing in common with Tarsus, which lay on a major east-west trade route and was home to the third-best university in the Greco-Roman world.

The doors that Nazareth and Tarsus opened to Jesus and Paul respectively certainly enlarged their minds, but they also permitted alien elements into their lives, which complicated the process of growing up. They both had to confront choices that did not present themselves to Jews in more sheltered environments.

The inner turmoil that Jesus and Paul had to live through brought each to a climax of frustration, which they both resolved in the same way. Each opted for a radical change of life-style that involved displacement. Jesus travelled south from Galilee to become a disciple of John the Baptist in Judea (Jn 3:22-24), while Paul travelled from Tarsus to Jerusalem to become a Pharisee (Gal 1:14; Phil 3:5). But that is not the end of the coincidences. After some time both realised that they were wrong in what they thought God was asking of them.

V

Christ as Model of the Preacher in the Teaching of Aquinas

LIAM WALSH, OP

CHRIST AS MODEL OF THE PREACHER IN THE TEACHING OF AQUINAS

Liam G. Walsh, OP

Thomas took his vocation as a preacher seriously: he fulfilled it in his daily work and he thought theologically about it in quite profound ways[1]. His profession as a Preacher gave him his distinctive way of living out the 'following of Christ'. It is in his thinking about Christ that his theology of preaching finds its fullest expression.

CHRIST AND PREACHING IN THE *SUMMA*

Thomas does his most explicit thinking about Christ in the Third Part of his *Summa theologiae (ST)*. But Christ has been present in his thinking all through the earlier sections of this work. His thinking about the mystery of God and God's creation in the First Part and his thinking about the human journey towards God in the Second Part have to find their verification in Christ, who unites the divine and the human in his own historical person. At the same time, the more abstract thinking of the first two Parts provides the presuppositions of the Third Part. Those presuppositions are the hermeneutical horizon in which Thomas interprets the Gospel accounts of Christ[2]. Some of these general presuppositions are about preaching. They come into play in Thomas's thinking about Christ the Preacher. To explore them is at once to learn what Thomas thought about preaching and what he thought about Christ. It is to learn how he could see Christ as the model for preachers.

1. For the place and significance of preaching in the life of Thomas see J.-P. Torrell, OP, *Saint Thomas Aquinas. Vol 1: The Person and His Work*, CUA Press, Washington DC, 1996, pages 69-74; also J.-P. Torrell, 'La pratique pastorale d'un théologien au XIIIe siècle. Thomas d'Aquin prédicateur' *Revue Thomiste* 82 (1982) 213-245

2. For an explanation of this movement of Thomas' theological thought in the *Summa* see Liam G. Walsh, OP, 'Sacraments' in *The Theology of Thomas Aquinas*, edited by Rik Van Nieuwenhove and Joseph Wawrykow, University of Notre Dame Press, 2005, pages 326-328

THE PRESENCE OF GOD IN HUMAN LIFE
(*SUMMA THEOLOGIAE* I.II)

One might start looking for principles that have a bearing on Thomas's understanding of preaching in the questions of the Second Part where he analyses the presence and action of God in the human search for beatitude. He sees this presence as two-pronged: God instructs humans by law and helps them by grace (I.II 90, prologue). God is the teacher of humans and his teaching takes the form of law; God is the co-mover present in all activity, and his presence within humans takes the form of grace. Neither instruction alone, nor the helping-hand alone, constitutes the presence of God in human life: one without the other will not get humans to God. The giving of law is done with words which, whether they come from God in revelation or from humans themselves in the elaboration of natural and positive law, put the call of God before the human mind. The giving of grace is done in the interior, subjective transformation of the spirit that allows humans to give themselves to God. These two features of the presence of God in human life have a Trinitarian ground. The Father sends (*missio*) Son and Spirit into the world for its salvation. The Son is Word, instruction, light. The Spirit is Love, gift, energy. Law corresponds to the Son, grace to the Spirit.

PROCLAIMING THE WORD

Law is a thing of words. Thomas's theological way of understanding law takes it beyond the formulation of legal codes. His view of it is not unlike the Jewish understanding of *Torah*. He is thinking about a *corpus* of spoken and written words that manifest God's covenant-related concerns for his people. In law they come to know God, hear his promises, are told of what God has done in fidelity to his promises, and learn what they should and should not do in order to inherit the blessedness that is promised.

The words of law are words that, in one way or another, carry authority. But they are also reasonable words. Law is an *ordinatio rationis*, 'a reasonable arrangement' of human behaviour (I.II 90, 1). In this view laws, in moving people, should be appealing to their sense of reasonableness. That people exercise their own reason and the freedom it grounds in their quest for God is the fundamental assumption of Thomas's analysis of human life in the Second Part of the *Summa*. If one is to find in God's giving of Law a paradigm for preaching, one will require preaching to be the speaking of a reasonable word.

THE WORD OF GOD

For Thomas, the key to understanding law theologically is its origin in the mind of God. God's eternal plan for bringing all the things God creates back to God is the *lex aeterna*, the eternal law (I.II 91, 1). All other law that comes to exist in created minds is an entry into the mind of God, whether it be the natural law that creatures discover to be written in their own being, or revealed law that comes from God, or human laws that people design for their own social well-being. All law is a bond between the thinking creature and the God who makes all things in God's Word and Wisdom. It follows, from this view of Thomas, that anyone who would claim to speak a word that binds others in their belief or behaviour must have somehow entered into the mind of God. At the very beginning of the *Summa* Thomas has presented theology as an entry into the inner mind of God (I 1, 7). The imperative that preaching requires the doing of theology, and of a theology that is contemplative wisdom, is very deeply rooted in his thinking. It is confirmed by the way he understands law.

LAW AND GRACE

Although Thomas distinguishes law from grace in the Prologue to question 90 of *ST* I.II, he never separates the two. He examines law as it functions in human salvation. Most of his analysis of law is, in fact, about the way it functioned historically in the Old and New Testaments. While Thomas's very detailed analysis of the Old Law is done primarily in terms of law, it is also an explanation of how the grace of God was present and active in the lives of the people who lived under the law. Law never brings justification without grace. Law guides people towards God in their external actions; it is grace that moves them interiorly to reach God (I.II 98, 1).

PROCLAIMING CHRIST

The grace that is present in the Old Law is the grace of Christ. Thomas asks in *ST* I.II 100, 1-2 whether the precepts of the Old Law justified people. He explains that they did, not precisely as precepts of law but because they put the coming of Christ before people, and thus brought them under the influence of his grace. Thomas sees the presence and the grace of Christ manifested particularly in the liturgical regulations of the Mosaic Law. But what he has to say there is valid for the entire corpus of the Old Testament. The period of the Mosaic Law is also the period of the prophets, as it is of the Psalms. The same prophetic word is present in Law, Prophets and Psalms. This is, of course, an important theological pointer to the preacher, who has to preach about the Scriptures of the Old as well as the New Testament. Every saving word recorded in the Scriptures as having binding force for God's people, has to be a word about Christ. This was how Christ himself interpreted the Scriptures.

THE NEW LAW

For Thomas the novelty of the New Law is not that it is about Christ, because the Old Law was already about him. The newness is the physical, historical presence of grace among God's people. With the coming of Christ there is the full, definitive outpouring of the Holy Spirit. In Christ and the Spirit the grace of God is visibly, tangibly present in the world. Thomas sets great store by this historical realism of the grace of God. The Holy Spirit is no longer given in transient interventions, contingent on the faith of those who reach out to the Christ who is to come. Christ has come once for all. He is glorified. In his glorification the Spirit is fully given. This Trinitarian fullness of divine presence in the world penetrates human interiority when no obstacle is put in its way, directing people from within towards God. In Christ law and grace coincide.

WRITTEN IN THE HEART, OF FEW WORDS

The first question Thomas asks about the New Law of the Gospel is whether or not it is a written law (I.II 105, 1). In his answer he will not entirely rule out some role for words and writing in the New Law. But he will give these a very secondary role. They must be subordinated to what is predominant (*potissimum*) in the law of the New Testament and gives it all its power. This is 'the grace of the Holy Spirit given by faith in Christ'. Thomas's argument for this position is taken straight from St Paul to the Romans (he quotes 3:27 and 8:2).

However, having established that the New Law is the inner grace of the Holy Spirit, he goes on in this first article about the New Law to concede that 'the New Law has, however, certain things that serve to dispose for the grace of the Holy Spirit and that touch the use of that grace. These have a kind of secondary place in the New Law. Those who believe in Christ have to be instructed in them, by the spoken and written word, both as regard what is to be believed and what is to be practised'. And so Thomas provides this nuanced conclusion: 'The New Law is principally a law given within, but in a secondary way it is a written law'. There is room still for a written Gospel and for the words of the preacher. If the written or spoken Gospel is a word of power, it is only because it is the proclamation of something that has already happened, and not just of something that is being waited for, and because it gives access to something that is actually present. The word of the preacher in the New Law is proclamation: anything it says will be drawing its power from the coming of Christ and the full outpouring of the Holy Spirit[3].

PREACHING AND THE COMMUNITY
(*SUMMA THEOLOGIAE* II.II)

Once Thomas has established how God is present in the human pursuit of beatitude, he can go on to examine, in *ST* II.II how humans seek God in their day to day living by the activity of the virtues and gifts and charisms that the grace of God underpins and the law of God guides. It is a life lived in the community of God's people[4]. After he has examined the virtues and gifts that are common to the life of all those being saved, he turns to the things that differentiate people within the community of those who journey together to God. A number of the things he says there have a bearing on what he thinks about preaching, and about Christ as the model of the preacher.

3. Thomas explains this as a difference between the Old and the New Law in I.II 101, 2 (in terms of revelation) and 103, 2 (in terms of sacraments).
4. While Thomas is primarily interested in the New Testament phase of that life, he examines it in sufficiently general terms to let what he has to say have a bearing on all phases of the history of God's People, on what the Fathers called the *ecclesia ab Abel*. He will concretise the things that are proper to the Christian dispensation more fully in the Third Part.

In the prologue to the first of the questions devoted to these matters (II.II 171) he explains the kinds of differentiations that have to be examined. There are differentiations according to charism (starting with prophecy), according to life-style (contemplative and active, and combinations thereof), and according to 'states of perfection'. On each subject he will have things to say that concern preaching.

PREACHING AND PROPHECY

The first differentiation that Thomas studies among the members of the Church is that coming from the charisms. While he refers to Paul's listing, he treats the charisms in an order of his own making. It is an order that is not unrelated to preaching, and not unrelated to the way he will analyse the ministry of Christ in the Third Part of the *Summa*. He thinks the charisms bear on three things: knowledge, speaking, and 'doing things' (*operationes*, which turn out to be miracles). Under the heading of knowledge he treats only of prophecy, saying that it includes the other charisms of knowledge. Indeed, the way he deals with it in II.II 171, 1 makes it draw also within itself the charisms of speaking and miracle working. The prophet is primarily someone who comes to know, by divine revelation, things that are remote from normal human knowledge, and specifically so because they pertain to the domain of the divine. But the prophet has also to be someone who speaks, because the knowledge that is given in prophecy is given for the building up of others. Furthermore, the prophet has to have the gift of miracle working, because the God-given truth that is to be announced cannot be confirmed by human reasoning but only by the power of God.

Not every preacher is a prophet. There are things in Thomas's analysis of the charism of prophecy that preachers dare not pretend to. But there are things said in it that offer suggestive parallels that can speak to the preacher. On the deepest level, the analogy of prophecy calls the preacher to enter into the mind of God. It is by being drawn into the mind of God by revelation that the prophet is able to claim that the word he or she speaks is the word of God to God's people. The preacher can do something analogous by prayer and by study. Then there are details that are at once comforting and challenging for the preacher. For example, Thomas asks in II.II 172, 4 whether moral goodness is required for prophecy. Having first established the negative answer from the way Paul separates prophecy from charity in 1 Corinthians 13, he confirms it by explaining: 'prophecy is given for the benefit of the Church, as are all the charisms, according to what Paul says in 1 Corinthians 12, 'to each is given the manifestation of the Spirit for the common good'; it is not directly ordained to making the heart of the prophet be united with God, which is what charity does'. That is a comforting thought for the preacher aware of his or her sinfulness. But Thomas adds immediately: 'If however we think of moral goodness in terms of human passions and concern with things outside oneself, then someone can be prevented from prophesying by moral wickedness. For prophecy requires the highest possible raising of the mind to the contemplation of spiritual things, and this is impeded by strong passions and undue concern with external things'. The preacher, no less than the prophet, has to be disposed for contemplation, and to be a contemplative, one must work at moral goodness.

PREACHERS AS CONTEMPLATIVES

Thomas's analysis of the contemplative and active ways of life is a reprise, with the addition of some Aristotelian up-dating, of the patristic tradition about contemplation and action, with the Martha/Mary typology at its heart. It is important to note that the subject of the discussion is not directly contemplation and action in themselves but *ways of life* dedicated to contemplation or to action. One can contemplate while not following a contemplative way of life, and one can follow a contemplative way of life and not be a contemplative. Thomas will use his understanding of these two ways of life, and combinations of them, when he comes to talk explicitly about preaching.

OFFICES AND STATES OF LIFE

It is in the questions on states and offices (*ST* II.II 183-189) that Thomas gives his most explicit attention to preaching. And it is from those questions that he will draw most clearly when he comes to study the life and ministry of Jesus. They are meant to be general questions about all human states and offices but they are in fact very much concerned with the actual distribution of states and offices in the Church of Thomas's day. He gives particular attention to issues raised by a debate about religious life that was lively in his own day. The form in which it was being lived by the Mendicant Orders, especially by Franciscans and Dominicans, was startlingly new and successful; and it was being strenuously objected to by sections of the secular clergy[5]. Thomas will defend this way of life primarily in the interests of the office of preaching. The other state of life he will examine is that of those who hold the office of Bishop. With them, too, he will give pride of place to preaching.

PERFECTION

In his questions about the New Law Thomas had explained how the Gospel is the definitive coming into the world of the grace of the Holy Spirit. The Christian dispensation, in its preaching, its sacraments and its structures, is the ultimate state of things. Everything that is needed for human perfection, for living the life of charity, is now available. The Spirit has been fully poured out, and the Church of Christ is and has everything that human salvation requires. Christians might not avail of all that is realised in Christ and the Church, but they cannot expect a better state of affairs to put things right for them. The only thing that has not yet been given is the coming of Christ in glory.

STATES OF PERFECTION

It is in relation to this ultimate, eschatological state of perfection that one must read the discussion about the states of perfection in questions 183-189 of *Summa theologiae* II.II. The three things from which Thomas justifies the diversity of offices and states that exist in the Church are the perfection of the Church, its universal effectiveness, and its consummate beauty (II.II 183, 2-3). The states represent the objective perfection of the Church. Not all its individual members represent it fully. In order to explain how it can be represented, Thomas draws on the distinction between three stages of spiritual progress that had become classical in spirituality: that of beginners, that of those making progress, and that of the perfect (II.II 183, 4). The perfect represent the eschatological fullness

5. On this see J.-P. Torrell, OP, *Saint Thomas Aquinas ...*, Vol.1, chapter 5

of grace; others represent states or stages of the journey towards it. It is from this that the idea of 'state of perfection' comes. It does not mean the state of those who are actually perfect – even if those who are in it ought to be perfect. It means the state of those who, in their form of life, represent what it is to occupy oneself with nothing else but being ready for the coming of Christ. Thomas has no difficulty remarking that 'there is nothing against some people being perfect who are not in the state of perfection, and some people being in the state of perfection who are not perfect' (II.II 184, 4).

BISHOPS AND RELIGIOUS

Aquinas examines two groups whom he considers to be in the state of perfection: Bishops and Religious. Bishops are in it by reason of their office. In the three stages of spiritual growth beginners and those making progress are enlightened by those who live the life that is proper to the perfect. The responsibility they have to enlighten others in the Church puts Bishops in the state of perfection. Religious are in the state of perfection because they have taken on, in a stable and solemn way (that is how Thomas understands the requirement for being in a 'state'), the obligation to do the things that manifest the ultimacy of the New Law. These are formulated in the Gospel as evangelical counsels. Those who oblige themselves, by a free choice, to practise the evangelical counsels (II.II 184, 3) separate themselves from the things of the world of time, and so put themselves into a state that expresses the perfection to which Christ calls all his disciples, which is the readiness for the coming of Christ. Those who put themselves in this state give stable expression to the way the whole Church needs to be detached from the things of time so as to be ready for the coming of Christ.

PREACHING AND THE STATE OF PERFECTION

Thomas makes a comparison between Bishops and those who live classical forms of religious life devoted to contemplation. He says the state of bishops is the more perfect of the two (II.II 184, 7). The reason he gives is that Bishops are 'perfecters', *i.e.* they are in a position that commits them to perfecting others, whereas religious, precisely as such, are committed to being perfect themselves. Religious are committed to the contemplative life, but bishops are committed to a way of life that suits a higher form of contemplation, which is to contemplate in view of instructing others (II.II 184, 7 *ad* 3). It is a distinctive way of contemplation that Thomas had already envisaged in his analysis of the contemplative and active lives (II.II 179, 1 *ad* 2). Thomas lists instruction first among the things expected of bishops (II.II 185, 3). The Bishop is a preacher. His state of life is that of contemplation issuing in preaching.

RELIGIOUS AS PREACHERS

Thomas takes it for granted that religious life can have contemplation as its goal, but feels the need to justify its taking as goals the works of active life (II.II 188, 2). Having explained how military service can be an appropriate goal for religious life (188, 3) he asks whether a way of religious life can be instituted for preaching and hearing confessions (188, 4). The question relates to the debate of his own day about the way of life of the Mendicants and specifically – through the reference to preaching – of his own Order.

Thomas makes his case for a way of religious life devoted to preaching by building on the legitimacy he has already established of a religious order being devoted to the pursuits of the active life. Preaching is a work of the active life. If religious orders can exist for goals like caring for the material needs of people and bearing arms for their defence, how much more can one exist that is devoted to serving the spiritual health of souls. In replying to objections Thomas is very specific that these religious preach and hear confessions within the authority, and even the economic structures, of the Church. He is talking about ecclesial preaching and reconciliation. He says that religious devoted to these goals are there to help those to whom these tasks belong *ex officio*, namely the bishops and other prelates (II.II 188, 4 *ad* 2).

PREACHING AND STUDY

Thomas follows his discussion on preaching as a goal for religious life with a question that reflects one of the novelties of his own Dominican way of life: could a way of religious life be established with studying as its goal (II.II 188, 5)? His positive answer, and the way he handles objections that come out of a strand of suspicion towards intellectual activity that has never been entirely absent from the Christian ascetical tradition, provide a framework for a real spirituality of study, at least for Dominicans[6]. Here it is enough to note how Thomas connects study with preaching. He says quite simply that 'the study of letters[7] is necessary in a religious way of life that is founded for preaching and other such activities' (188, 5 *ad* 2).

PREACHING AND CONTEMPLATION

Next he has to reconcile the primacy that the Christian tradition has always given to the contemplative life over the active life ('Mary has chosen the better part') with the way he is building up the spiritual value of the activity of preaching. In II.II 188, 6 he does it in an ingenious way that, if one did not know the rigorous objectivity of Thomas, one might take for a piece of Dominican chauvinism. He finds something in the active life of preaching that allies it to the contemplative life, and that makes it have the values of the contemplative life in a distinctive and eminent way. He finds it in the fact that teaching and preaching come from the fullness of contemplation. To speak about God one needs to be intimate with God. One must be a contemplative to preach in the way Thomas understands the term. If one is not, then what one is doing is simply not preaching.

On that basis Thomas goes on to make a comparison between the different forms of religious life (II.II 186, 6). He says that an active life of preaching and teaching is higher than a life devoted solely to contemplation: it is higher because it includes contemplation and adds to it an activity that itself flows from contemplation. He concludes quite simply that the highest form of religious life is that devoted to teaching and preaching. He clinches his conclusion by noting that this way of life is closest of all to the perfection found in the episcopate, which, for Thomas, remains the highest of all the forms of the state of perfection.

6. See Liam G. Walsh, OP, 'St Thomas and Study', in *La Formazione Integrale Domenicana, al servizio della Chiesa et della società*. A cura di Robert Christian OP, Edizione Studio Domenicano, Bologna 1996

7. He has used the word *studium* in a more generic sense of 'predominant thrust of one's life' to distinguish the active and contemplative ways of life in the prologue to II.II 171. He is more specific here in describing what we commonly understand as study as *studium litterarum*. But one would imagine he would want to keep the generic sense of *studium* even in this more specific use of the term.

CHRIST: PERFECTION IN THE FULLNESS OF TIME
(*SUMMA THEOLOGIAE* III)

The issue of perfection is very present in the Third Part of the *Summa*. Perfection exists in Christ – in his being, in his grace, in his knowledge, in his power. Because of the formal rigour of Thomas's analysis of Christ's perfection, the historical, existential side of his analysis does not stand out in the way it would in an historical theology. But from the first article he devotes to the Incarnation it is clear he is seeing the coming of Christ as the supreme and ultimate communication in time of God's goodness (III 1, 1). It is the ultimate, once-for-all event that brings salvation history to its fulfilment. It is in this eschatological perspective that one must understand Thomas's constant concern to establish the perfection of Christ. Perfection, as well as being formal excellence, is the achievement of finality[8]. It occurs in the fullness of time as well as in the fullness of being. It is in this existential perfection of grace (III 7), of knowledge (III 9-12), of power (III 13) that Christ is the supreme model for humans. It is the perfection of all the divine and human realities that Thomas has examined in general terms throughout the First and Second Parts of the *Summa*.

Thomas never separates Christ's personal perfection from his mission to be the Saviour of the world. It is among the basic set of reasons he gives, in III 7, 1 and elsewhere, for attributing the human perfection of habitual grace to Christ. The connection between his perfection and his mission appears, in a way that is particularly significant for preaching, in the explanation of why Christ had all the charisms: 'As was said in the Second Part, the charisms are ordained to the clear communication of faith and spiritual doctrine. The person who teaches has to have whatever it takes to communicate; otherwise their teaching comes to nothing. Now the first and originating teacher of spiritual doctrine and faith is Christ, according to Hebrews 2:3-4: 'How can we escape if we neglect so great a salvation? It was declared at first through the Lord, and it was attested to us by those who heard him, while God added his testimony by signs and wonders and various miracles, and by gifts of the Holy Spirit, distributed according to his will.'

8. *Summa theologiae* I 5, 1-3

Hence it is clear that all the charisms existed in the most excellent manner in Christ, as in the first and originating teacher of faith' (III 7, 7).

CHRIST'S WAY OF LIFE

Thomas is not satisfied to make only general statements about the perfection of Christ. He does a detailed study (that lasts from III 27 to III 59) of how that perfection was worked out existentially in the life of Christ that is presented in the Gospels[9]. It is in these questions that one can see most concretely how Christ is the model for preachers.

Having discussed the events of what he calls the entrance (*ingressus*) of Christ into our world, right up to his Baptism, Thomas presents a series of questions about how Christ actually lived among us (III 40-45). He starts with a section on what one might call the life-style of Christ. The question he asks are, it has to be recognised, very much influenced by the tradition of Christian spirituality he was living with, and with the dominant form of that tradition that was carried within religious life. However, even more influential in the portrait of Christ that emerges is the attention Thomas gives to preaching. Preaching is very much at the heart of the reasons he gives for understanding why Christ lived the way he did.

He asks first why Christ lived a public rather than a solitary life. The first reason he gives is that the Word was made flesh in order to give testimony to the truth, and to do that he had to live publicly, preaching publicly (III 40, 1). The other two reasons he gives also say something to the preacher. Christ came to save sinners, and so had to go out and find them, rather than sit around waiting for them to come to him. And he needed to make people comfortable about approaching him, so he mixed with them.

CONTEMPLATION AND ACTION

It is in reply to an objection that Thomas picks up the teaching about the active and contemplative life that he had established in the Second Part and uses it as a key for understanding Christ. He

9. See J.-P. Torrell, OP, *Le Christ et Ses Mystères. La vie et l'œuvre de Jésus selon saint Thomas d'Aquin. Tome I et Tome II* Desclée, Paris 1999

argues: 'The active life in which someone, by preaching and teaching, gives to others what he or she has contemplated is higher than a life given only to contemplation, because such a life supposes an over-flowing contemplation (*talis vita praesupponit abundantiam contemplationis*). And so Christ chose this way of life' (40, 1 *ad* 2). In his reply to the next objection, that was still urging the value of solitude, Thomas allows that Christ did at times go apart from people. The reasons given for his doing so are ones that speak to the preacher: his body needed rest in peace and quiet; he needed to give himself to prayer; he needed to avoid becoming too familiar with people who might try to manipulate him.

He again takes up the theme of preaching being the giving to others of what one contemplates in explaining why Christ did not live a particularly austere form of life (he ate and drank like others). In reply to an objection he recognises again that there was a place for solitude and fasting in the life of Christ, but that he left this behind when he went off to do what he came to do, which was to preach. The preacher can have times of solitude and of fasting, which are times for contemplation, but these practices must be left behind when it is time to preach (III 40, 2 *ad* 3).

POVERTY

Christ lived as a poor man. The reasons Thomas gives for that in III 40, 3 are all connected with preaching, the first very explicitly so: 'This was in keeping with the office of preaching, which was what he said he came for in Mark 1:38: "Let us go on to the neighbouring towns, so that I may proclaim the message there also; for that is what I came out to do". Preachers of the word of God should be entirely free from the care of worldly things – which they cannot be if they have riches – so that they can give themselves totally to preaching. And so the Lord himself, sending the Apostles said to them [quotes Matthew 10:9 and Acts 6:2]"'. As usual, he rounds out his position on the poverty of Christ in the replies to objections. Christ's poverty was voluntary, not imposed on him. It was poverty lived in sharing with others and being supported by benefactors. Such mendicant poverty, which entails living from a common table, allows one to have things in a way that does not impede the office of preaching (40, 3 *ad* 2).

TEMPTATIONS

Thomas devotes a question to the temptation of Christ (III 41). It is full of evocations of the human moral struggle, and of how Christ entered into it and was perfectly victorious in it. There is one gem for preachers in the text. An objector recalls that Thomas himself had said that Christ rightly did not live a life of notable austerity. In reply Thomas qualifies his position with this observation: 'No one should take on the office of preaching unless they are first purified and made perfect in virtue, as is said about Christ himself in Acts 1:1, "Jesus began to do and to teach". And therefore Christ, immediately after his baptism took on an austere form of life, in order to teach others that they should move on to the office of preaching only after they had subdued the flesh. As Paul said: "I punish my body and enslave it, so that after proclaiming (*praedicans* in Thomas's Latin text) to others I myself should not be disqualified (1 Corinthians 9:27).

PREACHING TO ALL PEOPLE

The question entitled 'On the Teaching of Christ' (III 42) deals with the range and method of Christ's preaching rather than with its content. Thomas wants to understand how Christ preached to all people even though he himself preached only to the Jews. In the background is Thomas's teaching about the passage from the Old Law to the New Law. He already touched on the issue of Christ's relationship to the Law in III 40, 4, when explaining why Christ lived according to the precepts of Jewish law. There, the second reason he gives is that Christ, 'in observing it would bring it to its consummation and to an end, showing that it was directed to himself'. The theme of fulfilment of the promises made to Israel is used again in III 42. But the argument is carried further by showing that Christ's preaching to the Jews was a first step towards the preaching of the Gospel to the Gentiles: the Jews were nearer to God in faith and worship than the Gentiles; it was appropriate that the teaching of Christ should be given first to them and through them to the Pagans.

PREACHING WITH POWER

Thomas offers another reason why Christ preached only to the Jews, and it is this: the event in which the New Law comes into being, which is the passion and death of Christ, had not yet occurred. Thomas will examine the theological significance of the passion further on in the Third Part. Here he invokes it to explain the power of Christ's preaching. It was by the victory of the cross that Christ merited power and lordship over the nations. It was only when that power was established – therefore after Christ's death on the cross – that salvation could be preached to the whole world. Christ showed his power over the nations, not by preaching to them himself but by sending out his disciples and giving them the power to teach the nations (III 42, 1, *ad* 1 & *ad* 2). It is the power that he gives to everyone who preaches in his name[10].

SPEAKING AND WRITING

That the power of preaching resides pre-eminently in the spoken word is affirmed by Thomas's explanation of why Christ did not give his teaching in writing (III 42, 4). His argument is that Christ is the supreme teacher. The best teachers have the power to imprint their teaching directly on the hearts of their disciples, without recourse to the medium of writing. Great teachers – he mentions Pythagoras and Socrates – did not write. The spoken words of Jesus had the power to go directly to the hearts of his disciples. He had no need to write. One has to relate this reasoning to what Thomas said in ST I.II 106 about the New Law of the Gospel not being a written law but being impressed on people's hearts by the grace of the Holy Spirit. Thomas recalls this teaching in his reply to the second objection: 'Because the Old Law was given in images that touched the senses it was appropriate that it should be written in signs that also touch the sense'. But the teaching of Christ, which is 'the law of the Spirit of life' (Romans 8:2), was to be 'written not with ink but with the Spirit of the living God, not on tablets of stone but on tablets of human hearts' (2 Corinthians 3:3). However, those who preach by writing can take encouragement from the fact

10. In the *ad* 2 Thomas gives a more descriptive analysis of how power was manifested in the preaching of Jesus: 'The power of Christ in teaching can be seen in the miracles by which he confirmed his teaching; in its persuasiveness; in the authoritativeness of its utterance, because he spoke as one having lordship over the Law, as when he said, "[you have heard] ...but I say to you"; and even in the influence of the correctness of his behaviour, living as he did without sin.'

that, as Thomas had conceded, there is a place for the written word in the New Law. He now recognises that Jesus arranged that his disciples should preach by both the spoken and the written word (42, 4, *ad* 3).

PREACHING WITH THE POWER OF MIRACLES

The preaching of Christ was accompanied by the working of miracles. In the First Part of the *Summa theologiae* I 105, 6-8 Thomas had established some basic principles about how God works miracles. He had subsequently examined the role of miracles in relation to the prophetic charism in *ST* II.II 171, 1 and 178, 1-2. The presuppositions carried over from there to the questions about Christ's miracles (III 43-44) are that only God can work miracles, although he may use humans, or angels as his instruments; and that God works miracles for two reasons: to confirm the truth of something that is being preached and to demonstrate the holiness of someone God wants to put forward as an example of virtue. Restated Christologically in III 43, 1, the two reasons for miracles are 'when someone does something that only God can do, the things that are being said can be believed to be from God' and 'to show the presence of God in a human person by the grace of the Holy Spirit; that is to say, when someone does the works of God it can be believed that God is dwelling in that person by grace, as is said in Galatians 3:5 "who gives you the Spirit and works miracles through you".' So Thomas concludes that Christ worked miracles in order to confirm his teaching and to show that God was present in him, by a grace that was not just of adoption but also of union.

FOR THE SALVATION OF THE WHOLE WORLD

The two reasons that Thomas gave for miracle-working often became separated in subsequent apologetical theology. Thomas sees them belonging closely together in Christ. What holds them together is their service to preaching. It is by the witness they give to the person of Christ that they confirm his teaching, a teaching that is primarily about his own person as the one in whom God comes in person to save his people. The miracles of Christ are, in fact, an integral part of the gospel proclamation that in him God is bringing the whole of the universe back to himself. This can be seen in the question Thomas devotes to the different kinds of miracles that Christ worked (*ST* III 44). The range and scale of the miracles are as wide as the universe itself. They include miracles worked on spiritual substances (angels and demons in 44, 1), and on the heavenly bodies (the sun and the sky and the stars, that were strangely disturbed at crucial moments in the life of Christ, in 44, 2). Then, there are the miracles, predominantly of healing, worked on human persons by which Christ 'showed that he is the universal and spiritual Saviour of all' (44, 3). And finally there are miracles worked on animals and plants (44, 4). The Gospel is a proclamation of the cosmic significance of Christ. The miracles are an intrinsic part of the message.

The preacher who would model himself or herself on Christ must have that appreciation of the cosmic power of the word given to them to speak. What is being announced in any sermon is the transforming power of the cosmic Christ. The word that does this has to be bold enough to take on the whole world. It is a word that conquers the powers of darkness, that makes the cosmos serve the Kingdom of God, that heals all human ills, that makes the earth and all it holds flourish and be beautiful. Good preachers have never feared to confront the demonic powers of evil, knowing that the word they speak conquers them. They have celebrated the cosmos and cared for the earth, because their word is a promise of the new creation. Above all they have practised and promoted human healing. Preachers have readily gathered around themselves women and men who devote themselves to the ministry of healing in all its forms, including the healing of minds through education. These are the daily 'miracles' that belong to the Gospel and confirm that God is in its teaching. Where preaching is done in that way – as in a religious family, for example, in which the work of preaching is accompanied by all the other works of the active life – it is more fully modelled on the preaching of Christ, who went around not just speaking but doing good. It moves the whole world towards the fulfilment of resurrection that awaits it at the return of Christ in glory.

VI

Eckhart on the Road to Damascus

DONAGH O'SHEA, OP

ECKHART ON THE ROAD TO DAMASCUS

Donagh O'Shea, OP

While some students of Eckhart's work have insisted on its contrast with St Thomas's, others have dwelt on their continuity. At the very least we can say that the primary thing these two Dominicans had in common was that both had spent their lives pondering and preaching the word. Both of them wrote extensive commentaries on various books of the Bible, but in their other works too the Scriptures are always decisively present. It is always the chosen Scriptural text that provides the key to understanding Eckhart's most obscure sermons (reversing, admittedly, the roles of text and sermon!).

I have often wondered what St Thomas's next work would have been like had Reginald of Piperno succeeded in persuading him, on that morning in 1273, to continue writing. But he was 'strangely altered,' and said, 'Reginald, I can write no more.' We would love to see how that strange alteration might have found expression in words. On his deathbed, at the insistence of the monks in Fossanova, he spoke about the Song of Songs – so he *was* open to persuasion. But it was not to be. Resisting at first the monks' request, he reminded them that their own St Bernard had commented at length on the Song of Songs. He could not fail to remember that Bernard had written there, 'The one who would know you, God, must measure you without measure.'

Meister Eckhart quoted this very phrase, along with several passages from the Song of Songs, in his sermon on Paul's spiritual experience on the road to Damascus[1]. It may be fanciful – but not entirely so – to expect that Thomas's next work might have exhibited some of the themes and even something of the style of Eckhart's sermons. It would not have been such a big step. Thomas (who quoted Dionysius the Areopagite seventeen hundred times in his written works) had a profound sense of the transcendence of

---

1. *Meister Eckhart, Sermons and Treatises*, translated and edited by M. O'C. Walshe, vol. 1., 1979, London and Dulverton (Watkins), p. 160

God. God cannot be comprehended, he said, because 'whatever is comprehended by a finite being is itself finite'[2].

The sermon about Paul's experience on the road to Damascus is one of Eckhart's more obscure. I can make no pretension to a scholarly treatment, but I would like to ruminate on this sermon for the space of a few pages.

RATIO AND INTELLECTUS

The text for this sermon is Acts 9:8, 'Paul rose from the ground and with open eyes saw nothing.' Eckhart immediately homes in on this 'nothing', turning it this way and that: 'The Nothing was God..., he saw nothing but God..., in all things he saw nothing but God..., when he saw God he saw all things as nothing.'

'God dwells in unapproachable light,' he quoted (1 Timothy 6:16). Light (he says 'fire') is invisible in itself, but it makes other things visible when it falls on them. This darkness that is light is a symbol of the 'Nothing' that is God, 'neither this nor that.'

The active intellect (what the medievals called *ratio*) relies on its ability to distinguish this from that, and so it is left outside. 'There is no way in to God. No one still on the way up, still on the increase in grace and light, ever yet got into God. God is not a growing light, yet one must have got to Him by growing. During the growing we do not see God. If God is to be seen, it must be in the light that is God Himself. A master says, "In God there is no less or more, no this or that." As long as we are on the approaches, we cannot get in.' This is more dramatic language than Thomas's, but the teaching is not different[3]. Quoting the Song of Songs, Eckhart says, 'Having passed on a *little* further, I found him that I sought.'

We speak of the degrees of knowledge, but these do not have degrees in turn ('knowledge of' not 'knowledge about'). I cannot

---

2. *Summa theologiae* I-II 4, 3 ad 1

3. 'Deum in hac vita non possumus perfecte cognoscere, ut sciamus de eo quid sit; possumus tamen cognoscere de eo quid non sit, ut Augustinus dicit [VIII *de Trinitate*, cap. II]; et in hoc consistit perfectio cognitionis viae' (*Quaestiones disputatae de caritate*, 10, *ad* 2 (contra). There are many statements to this effect throughout Thomas's work; see for example: *Summa theologiae* I 13, 10 ad 5; *In Boethii de Trinitate*, I, 2 *ad* 2 and *ad* 6; *Summa contra gentiles*, I,3 (premium); I, 5; I, 14

'almost' know the taste of a lemon. There is 'no way in'. I cannot 'almost' know what a circle is. Nine-tenths of a circle is not a circle. A Buddhist would say you cannot be 'almost' enlightened. I cannot 'almost' know God: nothing is 'almost' God. God is simple: 'God is not a growing light.' This would appear to end in agnosticism, leaving no way of coming to knowledge of God. If there is no way in, what significance can our efforts have? But try we must, knowing that all our efforts must end in failure. 'One must have got to God by growing,' he says. We cannot just sit and wait for understanding; we have to struggle to know God. But knowledge of God is not the result of our efforts. It is a gift from God. 'If God is to be seen it must be in the light that is God.' This light is not accessible to *ratio*. But 'above the intellect that seeks there is another intellect which does not seek, but stays in its pure, simple being, which is embraced in that light.' It is what the medievals called *intellectus*[4].

'*Above* the intellect that seeks...', he said. Medievals could not speak of two things without placing one above the other: *nobilior* was a word that came readily to them. In feudal society everything was hierarchical: all power came from above. They projected this onto everything: the heavenly bodies were made of material that was 'more noble' than earthly material, certain human faculties were 'higher' than others, *etc*. Eckhart constantly used the spatial image

---

4. Allowing for Eckhart's preaching style, there is no reason to believe that he differed from Thomas on this point. Thomas, like all the medievals and the philosophers of antiquity, saw *ratio* as the essential factor in human knowledge; but he allowed that we also have a certain participation in a higher kind of knowledge, and quoted Dionysius at length in support. 'Quamvis cognitio humanae animae proprie sit per viam rationis, est tamen in ea aliqua participatio illius simplicis cognitionis quae in substantiis superioribus invenitur, ex quo vim intellectivam habere dicuntur' (*Quaest. disp. de veritate*, 15, 1). He stresses that *ratio* and *intellectus* are not separate faculties. 'Non est...in homine aliqua potentia a ratione separata, quae intellectus dicatur; sed ipsa ratio intellectus dicitur, quod participat de intellectuali simplicitate, ex quo est principium et terminus in eius propria operatione' (*ibid.*). Eckhart speaks in sermon 19 of the participation of *ratio* (and the other faculties) in *intellectus*, rather than of any separation between them: 'All the soul's powers are lifted up and exalted: the outer senses we see and hear with, and the inner senses we call thoughts....' 'The intellect that does not seek [...] is pure light in itself. This light embraces in itself all the powers of the soul.'

'height', but he was not in fact held captive by it: 'height and depth,' he said, 'are one'.[5] Today, without loss of meaning, we might say instead that *intellectus* is *deeper* than *ratio*, or at the *heart* of it.

Alas for *intellectus* today. 'Knowledge is power,' wrote Francis Bacon almost four centuries ago. A few years later Descartes declared that by means of science we can become 'masters and owners of nature.' Then a little more than two centuries ago Kant wrote: 'Reason acquires its possessions through work.' Knowledge here becomes production; reason 'knows only that which it brings forth according to its own design.' All knowledge, said Kant, is discursive: the work of reason lies in deducing, demonstrating, distinguishing, comparing, relating, abstracting. He identified mind with *ratio*, and rejected as delusion the intuitive or contemplative vision of *intellectus*. We live still in a mental world shaped by scientists and philosophers who made contemplation impossible in principle.

The value, as well as the challenge, of reading Eckhart is that he pre-dated this development. Without decrying the place of *ratio*, thus plunging us into false mysticism, he speaks to us of its limits, and shows us how to conduct ourselves when we touch those limits. It is not by cutting off theology that we enter on the contemplative path. Neither is it by attempting to bypass prayer, asceticism, ritual, liturgy, work. Rather, these are the preludes to contemplation, and its place-holders; without them there is no context, no guidance, no way of integrating the experience in our life. Contemplation dawns in the deepest part of them or at the heart of them (but not predictably like the dawn; it usually has to break in). 'With *open* eyes he saw all things as naught.'

UNION WITH GOD

Thomas is the specialist in holding everything in place. At times he is almost too irenic for us. True, in every article of every question there is the brief engagement of objection and reply, but he is always sure of the outcome in advance (at the time of writing, at least), and the conclusion is there because it 'fits'. With Eckhart there is a sense of rupture and drama; and yet things manage to hold together. His sermons echo his own arduous path, and ours.

5. 'Talks of Instruction,' n. 23, in *Sermons and Treatises*, vol. 3, p. 53

The most hardened self-will is the self-will of the mind. It is harder than any material substance, yet it is made only of thoughts – nothing! It is this that has to break on the rocks in meditation (or 'contemplation', to give it its old name). It was when Paul was busy with judgement, 'breathing threats and murder,' that he 'fell to the ground.' Only then did the light from heaven flash around him. And when he arose, with open eyes he saw Nothing. He was plunged into the most poverty-stricken kind of knowing. In the words of another Eckhart sermon, *Beati pauperes*, he was 'made free of all the understanding that lived in him.'

The rational mind distinguishes, compares, and contrasts 'this and that'. Or rather it distinguishes *concepts* of this and that, omitting other considerations. In the act of doing so it disregards what this and that have in common, thus eclipsing their underlying unity. It is perfectly legitimate to do this for some purpose, but in meditation there is no purpose. In the heart of darkness Paul heard a voice saying to him, 'Saul, Saul, why do you persecute *me*?' In that darkness Jesus is not distinguished from his disciples; they are one. In that darkness there is only unity. To meditate is to stand resolutely in that unity. The mind is not distinguished from the body, the self is not distinguished from the other, the disciple is not distinguished from the Master, the creature is not distinguished from the Creator[6]. *Ratio*, interrupting at this point, would call this monism or pantheism; but this is beside the point. All the distinctions still obtain. They are not being denied, now or ever, but they are not being made just at that moment. All such charges against Eckhart, and orthodox mysticism generally, stem from a confusion of *ratio* and *intellectus*.

6. In *The Little Book of Truth*, Henry Suso offers a clarification of Eckhart's teaching on this point: 'Man can be one [with God] in a certain sense when he loses himself in God, in losing himself while outwardly seeing, enjoying, and the like. I shall give an analogy of this. The eye loses itself while seeing because in the act of seeing it becomes one with its object, yet each remains what it is ... The soul always remains a creature. But when it is lost in the Nothing it is not at all aware of how it is a creature or how it is nothing, or whether or not it is a creature, or whether it is united or not': *Henry Suso: The Exemplar, with Two German Sermons*, translated and edited by Frank Tobin, (Classics of Western Spirituality Series), 1989 New York, Paulist Press, p. 321

Eckhart's most challenging words, 'Let us pray to God that we may be free of God' (*Beati pauperes*), are understood in this light. The second 'God', in that phrase, is the Creator, and is therefore distinguished, by *ratio*, from the creature. While never wanting to play this down, Eckhart wants to stand in the original unity. All creatures exist from all eternity in the mind of God, according to the Platonic teaching (accepted also by St Thomas); but, according to the medieval axiom, everything in God is God; or as Eckhart put it, 'in God there is nothing but God.' So, in the mind of God all creatures are one with God. 'While I yet stood in my first cause [before he came to be], I had no [creator] God.' His invitation is to stand in that unity, even now, since it is our deepest identity.

If 'unity' seems too strong a word to describe the contemplative moment, we can try 'presence'. Just as 'unity' does not exclude distinction (in accordance with *ratio*), presence does not exclude this unity. It might appear to do so, for *ratio* comes in with a question, 'But what am I present to?' There are no innocent questions. Under the guise of a question it is insinuating a distinction between a 'what' and an 'I'. But here there is just presence. *Ratio* gives a legitimate view from the outside, but contemplation is the inside of the experience itself. In that experience there is no separate self. This is true of any experience even loosely called contemplative. We can lose our sense of separation as we contemplate a sunset, or a forest, or a loved one; or when we hear great music. Why should we be keen to exclude this from our religion? Of course, just as there is a higher merging of the self, there is also a lower: you can witness mob frenzy on television, or on the street; or you can talk to an adept about alcohol or drugs. So it is nothing unusual in itself. It is here that the necessity of *ratio* is seen: it distinguishes sane from crazy mysticism. But when we have settled that issue, why should we remain forever outside thinking and talking about the presence of God? We are invited to enter the Presence.

If there is no 'I', neither is there a 'what'. Only to *ratio* is God an object. 'It appeared to a man as in a dream – it was a waking dream – that he became pregnant with Nothing like a woman with child, and in that Nothing God was born, He was the fruit of Nothing. God was born in the Nothing.' O'C. Walshe adds a note to this: 'I think it is the record of a personal experience. Eckhart probably uses the third person form just as St Paul does in 2 Corinthians 12:2ff.' A Zen friend has no hesitation in reading this as Eckhart's description of an enlightenment experience – *kensho* or *satori* – in which, to use the Scholastic word, *intellectus* became wide awake in him, no longer the flickering thing it usually is.

I am always inside something. If I am not inside the presence of God I am inside the experience of thinking about the presence of God. The activity of thinking arises from a source that is not thinking. Where is my ultimate home, my source? What am I when I am not thinking? Ask Descartes and see him at a loss. I am afraid that I may be nothing. *Ratio* is just the best dressed of a host of activities (imagination, remembering, planning, day-dreaming...) that seem to offer a safety net above an abyss of emptiness. In meditation all this mental furniture and its uses can be glimpsed, vaguely at first, and then more clearly as the years go by. Eventually I get glimpses of the room itself. 'At stroke of midnight soul cannot endure / A bodily or mental furniture' (W.B. Yeats). I get the grace to see that this room is not my home. It is my ego, my own construction; it is not my deepest identity.

'Why does she say [in the Song of Songs], "Him my soul loves"...? She did not name Him she loved. There are four reasons why she did not name Him. One reason is that God is nameless ... God is above all names. The second reason ... is that when the soul swoons away into God with love, she is aware of nothing but love ... The third reason is, she had no time to name Him. She cannot turn away from love for long enough to utter another word but 'love'. The fourth is, perhaps she thinks He has no other name but 'love'. With 'love' she pronounces all names...'

There are many synonyms for love, and most of them wear thin with use. *Agapè* is not a household word, and the trouble starts when we try to find an English equivalent. Perhaps for a moment we could tolerate a cumbersome phrase: to love is 'to be one with'. This has the advantage of being at once general and practical. It does not have to be extricated from the dense language of emotions; and it can apply just as well to washing a mug as to contemplating God. 'To be one with' is to give yourself, body and soul, holding nothing back. To be one with everything you do while you are doing it – not watching yourself doing it, not judging and checking, remaining subtly withdrawn – this is to live in love. If you do that all day, your meditation will be much clearer and simpler and not essentially different from everything else you do. 'Paul rose from the ground,' said Eckhart, 'and with open eyes saw nothing. I cannot see what is one.'

A monk from Gethsemani Abbey visited our priory, and as I led him upstairs to the guestroom I apologised for the long climb. 'Don't worry about that,' he said, 'there are many steps in Gethsemani Abbey too … I always count them as I go up.' When I asked how many there were, he said, 'I don't know! Here's how I count them: *one, one, one….*' It was a lesson in contemplation. To count in the usual way is to stand apart from the action itself, measuring progress. But 'I cannot see what is one.' I cannot count what is one. Strange that the German mystics, who had so much analytical power, spoke so little about stages and methods in the spiritual life. 'A famous teacher,' said Tauler, referring to Eckhart, 'spoke of … the way to God which has no way and the manner of finding Him which has no manner'.[7]

THE WAY THAT IS NO WAY

'The soul…has come home and dwells in her simple, pure light. There she does not love…' Eckhart appears now to erase the very thing he has used to erase all else. It may appear inconsistent with itself, but it is his consistent teaching. 'You must give up yourself, altogether give up self, and then you have really given up … Alas! how little and how paltry are the things you have given up. It is blindness and folly, so long as you care a jot for what you have given up. But if you have given up self, then you have really given up'.[8] To give oneself up is to give up (especially) one's spiritual 'attainment'. What he said in Sermon 17 about justice applies equally to love: 'The one who is devoted to justice is taken up by justice, seized of justice, becomes one with justice.' To love is not to

7. *Spiritual Conferences,* translated and edited by Eric Colledge and Sr M. Jane, 1978 Rockford, Illinois, Tan Books and Publishers, p. 238
8. Sermon 18, M. O'C. Walshe, *op. cit.,* vol. 1, pp. 142f

count or calculate but 'to be one with'. Suso, struggling with himself, wrote, 'It is detachment above all detachment to be detached in one's detachment[9]. It is a needed warning; the ego has a subtle palate and fattens particularly on spirituality.

This 'way that is no way' is open to misunderstanding, of course, and it holds a special appeal for short-cutters and lazy people. Even in the 14th century, evidently, there were people who were willing to 'hang loose' and wait to see what would come their way. 'There was one great teacher,' said Tauler, 'who taught you and told you about these things, but you did not understand him ... Many people applied what he said to the lower stages of prayer, and so they went horribly astray.' This was most probably a reference to the Brethren of the Free Spirit, a loose association of people (or perhaps just a climate of opinion) who believed that the contemplative way absolved them from all religious practices – prayer, liturgy, asceticism, even morality. Eckhart was blamed by some for being the main inspirer of this movement, and it is interesting to see both Tauler and Suso coming to his defence. A simple check would have shown how misplaced was the charge: 'Now someone might say, "Well ... why should I have to strive so hard and be so detached? I will have the right to be a good man, and take my ease, and I will have as good a share of heaven as those who struggle for it". To this I say: Just as far as you are detached from things, you possess them, and no more. But if you think of what you may get, and have your eye on it, then you will get nothing'.[10]

9. *Little Book of Eternal Wisdom*, Suso, *op.cit.*, p. 234. This is more commonplace than it sounds. 'A perfect abandonment must even go so far as to abandon its abandonment' wrote François Fénelon to Madame Guyon; and for those who care, there are many Zen stories to the same effect. Thomas Merton's inspired 'translation' of Chuang Tzu has this: 'In the age when life on earth was full, no one paid any special attention to worthy people ... They were honest and righteous without realizing that they were 'doing their duty.' They loved each other and did not know that this was 'love of neighbour.' They deceived no one yet they did not know that they were 'men to be trusted.' They were reliable and did not know that this was 'good faith.' They lived freely together giving and taking, and did not know that they were generous. For this reason their deeds have not been narrated. They made no history': *The Way of Chuang Tzu*, 1965 New York, New Directions Publishing Corporation, p. 76

10. O'C Walshe, *op. cit.*, vol. 2, p. 203

There is widespread interest in meditation/contemplation today among ordinary Christian; groups abound everywhere. Among Church authorities there is generally less enthusiasm: nervousness, rather. This is consistent with experience of days gone by[11] and I suspect that it often has more to do with fear than with faith. Not all contemplatives are proficient in canon law! Nor are they always skilful at explaining themselves; they can sometimes say foolish or shocking things. They become sitting targets for rationalistic theologians who have scant regard for *intellectus*. This speaking to different purposes is obvious in the charges brought against Eckhart near the end of his life. Law has a way of trying to become spirit, attempting to enter every nook and cranny where only spirit can penetrate.

Real contemplatives have the power to unmask our anxious certainties. The 13th century mystic, Blessed Angela of Foligno, had a deep experience of God, and when her confessor asked her to tell him about it, she said, 'Father, if you experienced what I experienced and then you had to stand in the pulpit to preach, you could only say to the people, "My friends, go with God's blessing, because today I can say nothing to you about God"'.[12] This might seem to leave preachers with little to do. But it is just this state of the deepest poverty that gives value to their words. While *ratio* rightly treasures its riches, *intellectus* enters the poverty of unknowing. "There must be a stillness and a silence for this Word to make itself heard. We cannot serve this Word better than in stillness and in silence: there we can hear it, and there too we will understand it aright – in the unknowing. To the one who knows nothing it appears and reveals itself".[13]

11. See, for example, the series of articles on the Quietist controversy by James Kelly in *Spirituality*, Dominican Publications, Dublin, vol. 4, no. 20, 1998, pp 316-319; no. 21, 1998, pp. 351-354; vol. 5, no. 22, 1999, pp. 30-33; no. 23, 1999, pp. 91-94; no. 24, 1999, pp. 165-169

12. Quoted in Raniero Cantalamessa, *La Parola e la Vita: Riflessioni sulla Parola di Dio delle Dominiche e delle Feste dell'anno: Anno C*, 1993 Roma, Città Nuova Editrice, p. 96

13. Sermon 2, O'C. Walshe, *op. cit.*, vol.1, p.21

VII

'Get into the River':
The Dominican Passion for Study

VIVIAN BOLAND, OP

'GET INTO THE RIVER':
THE DOMINICAN PASSION FOR STUDY[1]

Vivian Boland, OP

The Dominican historian Simon Tugwell was giving a series of lectures to Dominican Sisters in Rome on the essential elements of Dominican religious life. On the first day he spoke about obedience, on the second day he spoke about poverty, and so the sisters were confident that they knew what he would speak about on the third day. And they were quite looking forward to hearing what he would have to say about the subject. So on the third morning he began: 'I have already spoken about obedience and I have spoken about poverty, and today I want to say something about the other essential element of Dominican religious life, study'.

In speaking about study he is, of course, speaking about passion and love and desire, since the Latin *studium* means passion, love, desire, concern. Things that attract our interest and engage our energies become the objects of our study. The things to which we devote time and thought are the objects of our *studium*. They are the things about which we are passionate, for which we are eager to work.

Simon Tugwell was also being faithful to an important change in the revised Dominican Constitutions where study is now treated under 'the following of Christ' and not under 'formation' where it had been dealt with before. At the beginning of his Letter on the role of study in the Order, Damian Byrne drew attention to the significance of this change:

> The 'Gillet' Constitutions (1930) gave the impression that study was linked to the first years of Dominican life, a necessary preamble to a life of preaching and ministry. Whole generations of Dominicans have been affected by this attitude. The River Forest Constitutions (1968) restored the tradition that study and reflection are an integral part of our religious tradition, yet the earlier spirit persists among many who see

1. An earlier version of this paper was delivered at the annual meeting of European Dominican Provincials held at Kiev, Ukraine in 2005. It has benefited from discussions there as well as from suggestions made by Paul Murray OP.

study as being confined to specialists, or [to] a particular period of our lives as Dominicans[2].

Timothy Radcliffe's 1995 Letter developed this understanding of study as an integral part of our religious tradition and a *permanent* element in the life of any Dominican[3]. Study is not just something that some of us do, or something we all do for a short period, but something that must be part of our lives always if we are to be what we aspire to be, preachers of the Word of God. This approach to study has continued to inform the Acts of recent General Chapters, in particular that held at Providence, Rhode Island in 2001.[4]

The argument in this paper is as follows. A review of the main features of Dominican education in the formative decades of the Order's life leads into a summary of continuity and change in the Order's subsequent legislation about study – here I will be even more brief. In the second half of the article some contemporary questions are identified, in responding to which, it is argued, the Dominican passion for study has crucial things to offer.

THE DOMINICAN EDUCATIONAL SYSTEM

The decision of the River Forest Chapter (1968) is a genuine return to the original inspiration that led to the establishment of the Order and is fully supported by recent research on Dominican education in the first century of the Order's life. The tendency has been, when we think about study in the context of the Order's tradition, to look to the 13th century, to revisit the sources of the Order's coming to be and to compare ourselves with what we find there. The tendency has been also, to look to the highest mountain peaks in that whole movement of Dominican education in the 13th century, as regards places, to look to Paris and Oxford, and as regards people, to look to Albert the Great and Thomas Aquinas.

Paris and Oxford were the great centres of theological learning in the Middle Ages and the Order quickly established a strong

2. Damian Byrne OP, 'On the role of study in the Order' (1991) now available in *To Praise, To Bless, To Preach: Words of Grace and Truth*, Dominican Publications, Dublin 2004, pages 267-76. The quotation is from page 268.

3. Timothy Radcliffe OP, 'The Wellspring of Hope: Study and the Annunciation of the Good News', in *To Praise, To Bless, To Preach: Words of Grace and Truth*, Dominican Publications, Dublin 2004, pages 349-74

4. Acts of the General Chapter of Providence, Rhode Island (Rollebon Press, Tallaght, Dublin, §§104-201 [pp.45-70].)

presence and involvement in the life of these budding universities. And of course Albert and Thomas stand high above all others in the thirteenth century as students and teachers of theology. One danger in focusing on these exceptional places and people is that we get depressed when we see how feeble our own efforts are by comparison. A more serious danger is that we will misunderstand the role of study by failing to appreciate the whole system of Dominican education that developed very quickly and whose inspiration was not a desire for academic glory or ecclesiastical power but simply the desire to preach well. The Order's great intellectuals were teachers in the first place, looking to the needs of their students and of the Church at large. Neither should we underestimate what is involved in preaching well. Humbert of Romans, Master of the Order from 1254 to 1263, says that 'preaching cannot be done worthily without immense difficulty'.[5]

Marie Michèle Mulchahey is a student of the renowned Irish Dominican medievalist Leonard Boyle. In her recent book 'First the Bow is Bent in Study': Dominican Education before 1350,[6] she shows that in the early decades of the Order's life every Dominican convent was a house of studies. Each convent had its lector, and the friars, without exception, were expected to attend his lectures each day. These lectures very quickly came to be appreciated by others, and there is evidence of bishops wanting Dominican foundations to be made in their dioceses in order to provide theological education for their clergy[7]. Having a Dominican priory in the diocese meant that you automatically also had a school, since

5 Humbert's Treatise on Preaching has much to say about study. An English translation edited by Walter M.Conlon OP was published by Blackfriars Publications, London in 1955. A more recent translation by Simon Tugwell OP is available in his Early Dominicans: Selected Writings, Paulist Press, New York and Mahwah 1982, pages 179-370. The quotation is from paragraph 98 of Humbert's treatise (Conlon trans., p. 36; Tugwell trans., pp. 209-10).

6 M. Michèle Mulchahey, First the Bow is Bent in Study: Dominican Education before 1350 Studies and Texts132, Pontifical Institute of Mediaeval Studies, 1998. See also Tugwell, Early Dominicans, pages 24-27 and Louis Bataillon OP, 'Le rapport entre l'étude et la prédication chez les frères prêcheurs au XIIIème siècle', in La Formazione Integrale Domenicana al Servizio della Chiesa e della Società Edizioni Studio Domenicano, Bologna 1996, pages 95-102.

7 Mulchahey, First the Bow..., pp 50 & 52 (for the dioceses of Metz, Liège and Bourgogne).

the Dominicans themselves studied together in their convents every day. Thomas Aquinas is the only Dominican we know of, in the thirteenth century, who was allowed (not without a struggle) to move directly from being a student to being a lecturer at Paris without first cutting his teeth as a conventual lector[8]. The custom was that Dominican teachers worked their way from conventual lector, to teaching in provincial houses of study, and then perhaps to the Order's *studia generalia*, its international houses of study. Albert the Great, was conventual lector in four or five priories of his province before he was asked to teach at Paris.

Between the individual convents and the great international *studia generalia* of the Order, there was an intermediate level of provincial *studia*. These provincial houses of study provided more intensive courses in Scripture and theology. Sometimes, depending on different needs from time to time and from place to place, such provincial *studia* focussed on biblical studies, languages, logic, or natural philosophy. Under the impulse of Albert, and his reading of Aristotle's *Ethics*, moral philosophy became a key part of the curriculum of provincial *studia*, and it fell to the master of students to give the lectures in moral philosophy. At Santa Sabina, Thomas Aquinas was given his head in designing a curriculum for pastoral and moral theological education, the fruit of which is his famous *Summa theologiae*.[9]

Any Dominican teacher, it seemed, had to be ready to move around within the different elements of the Order's educational system. Thomas, for example, finished a term at Paris, then worked as conventual lector, was next asked to set up a *studium personale* at Santa Sabina, returned to Paris for a second term, and finally came back to his province to help setting up a provincial *studium* at Naples. The point of recalling the course of Thomas's career is to give a sense of how the Order's educational system was multi-layered and how even its most eminent theologian was ready to serve the needs of the Order at whatever level he was asked to.

Mulchahey's thesis is that Dominican education, and the role of study in the Order's life, is misunderstood if we start at the top

8. Mulchahey, *First the Bow ...*, pages 383-84
9. See Leonard Boyle OP, *The Setting of the Summa theologiae of Saint Thomas*, Toronto 1982

and is only properly understood if we start at the bottom, at the level of each priory which was also meant to be a school. Even if nobody else came to study at a particular priory, the friars themselves would be attending classes. Their work was preaching, teaching, and guiding souls, and their conviction was that such work could not be done effectively if they were not always also studying. Leonard Boyle himself summarised it as follows:

… every Dominican house was geared to study in the interests of the pastoral care and was supposed to have its own Lector to look after the instruction of the community. And even after the younger *fratres communes* had become priests and were engaged in preaching and counselling, only an *ad hoc* dispensation could excuse them from attendance at the Lector's classes. In this sense the *fratres communes* were forever *iuniores* and always in need of being brought up to date, the better to advance their *cura animarum*.[10]

Of course the younger members of the Order needed an initial education in the Scriptures and in theology. They were taught in the novitiate that study would be a permanent part of their way of life and one of the goals of the novitiate was that they would develop the dispositions required for diligent study. The *Primitive Constitutions* charge the master of novices to teach those in his charge how earnest they must be in their study, always reading or thinking about something by day and by night, in the house or when they are on a journey, and striving to retain as much as they can in their minds[11].

The overall impression that emerges from Mulchahey's survey of the Order's educational system between 1220 and 1350 is of how committed the Order was to providing the best possible education for its members in order to sustain them in their work of preaching, teaching, and guiding souls. Great administrators and great scholars, provincial and general chapters, all worked together to

10. Leonard Boyle OP, 'Has the Dominican Order accepted the Integral Formation conceived by St Thomas?', in *La Formazione Integrale Domenicana al Servizio della Chiesa e della Società* Edizioni Studio Domenicano, Bologna 1996, pages 23-30. The quotation is from page 25.

11. Simon Tugwell, OP, *Early Dominicans*, page 466

adapt and to strengthen the Order's life of study. The collaboration of Humbert of Romans and Albert the Great is particularly noteworthy[12].

It is not that the Order had a twofold purpose, preaching and study, but that it had a single purpose, preaching for the salvation of souls. Everybody was clear that preaching for the salvation of souls simply could not be done without study. 'First the bow is bent in study', the title of Mulchahey's book, is from a comment of the Dominican scholar and later Cardinal, Hugh of Saint-Cher. He takes the rainbow that appeared in the sky after Noah's flood (Genesis 9) as an image of preachers full of refreshing and life-giving water, poised to pour it over the earth. 'First the bow is bent in study', Hugh says, thinking now of the bow that fires arrows, ' and then the arrow is released in preaching'. Just as the archer needs both bow and arrows if he is to hit the mark, so the preacher needs study and preaching if he is to be effective in his work. Study, Simon Tugwell says, 'is a matter of life and death for the preacher'.[13]

'WHAT SO OFTEN HAS BEEN CONFIRMED IN VIEW OF THE ORDER'S PURPOSE' (General Chapter, Rome 1694)[14]

The centrality of study is clear then from a review of the early decades of the Order's life. General and provincial chapters, as well as Masters of the Order, showed great ingenuity and flexibility in adapting institutional arrangements to different situations, all at

12. Mulchahey, First the Bow..., page 145: 'Albert the Great is perhaps the pivotal figure from about 1245 in the debate over the place of philosophy, and Aristotelian thought in particular, in the work of the theologian'. In 1262, when Albert's commentaries on Aristotle's texts were just about complete, Humbert sanctioned the Order's first studium naturarum, 'school of natural philosophy' (Mulchahey, page 262). The collaboration of Albert and Humbert deserves to be better known.

13. Tugwell, Early Dominicans, page 24. For Hugh's comment on Genesis 9:13 see Mulchahey, First the Bow..., pages ix and 553.

14. ... toties ab initio Ordinis constituta sunt, inspecto Instituti nostri fine (Fontana, Constitutiones ..., page 42). For this, and other references to the legislation of General Chapters, see Vincentius Fontana OP, Constitutiones, Declarationes et Ordinationes Capitulorum Generalium S.O.F.P. ..., Rome 1862, a thematic gathering of the acts of General Chapters from 1221 to 1844. It should be noted that such legislation is not necessarily a record of how Dominicans actually lived as much as an indication of how they thought they ought to be living.

the service of the Order's mission of preaching for the salvation of souls.

Taking a longer view of the Order's tradition, other aspects are just as clear. The Order has always gone to great lengths to promote study, to protect its pursuit, and to facilitate those of its members who were charged with particular responsibilities in relation to study. Sometimes this can be seen negatively, in the sanctions imposed on priors, and others, who failed to meet their responsibilities concerning study. Students who do not study, who fall asleep in class, or who absent themselves from lectures: are all subject to penalties. Visitators are to see that the brethren are diligent in study. Sanctions ranged from withdrawal of the wine ration for minor offences, to incarceration in the conventual dungeon for brothers who fall into heresy[15].

The story is not all rosy, even in the golden age of the Order's beginnings. Already in his encyclical letter of May 1233 Jordan of Saxony, Saint Dominic's successor as Master of the Order, laments that many superiors are not concerned about study and that lectors in some places are so half-hearted about their job and give lectures so reluctantly and infrequently that it is no wonder the students become even more unenthusiastic than their unenthusiastic teachers[16].

The Order's support of study is also seen positively in a number of ways. General chapters are very concerned, for example, with books and with what happens to the books of dead Dominicans. They are concerned with protecting the library as a space in which study can be undertaken and which should not therefore be used for any other purpose. It is recognised that study requires time and space. Masters of students are to ensure that good cells are assigned to those who will use them well for study. Priors are to

15. Fontana, *Constitutiones* ..., page 455, section 5 (withdrawal of wine); page 464, section 26 (dungeon).

16. Tugwell, *Early Dominicans*, page 123. As well as reluctant teachers, Jordan identifies two other problems concerning study. Many superiors are unconcerned about study to the extent that they take gifted people away from it in order to put them doing other jobs. And there is general laziness among the brethren who fail to appreciate the link between their study and the salvation of people's souls (pages 123-24).

dispense brothers from other duties, even liturgical ones, in order to facilitate study[17]. Provincials are to send suitable friars to places where study is flourishing. Troublesome and grumpy students are not to be sent, says the General Chapter of 1251, only those who are apt for studies and are mature in their morals.

In the first century of its life, perhaps in this contrasting with recent experience, it is simply accepted that the friars will be prepared to travel in order to study, just as they will be prepared to travel in order to teach. Each province had the right to send students to Paris and to the other *studia generalia* of the Order. When the Oxford community sought to exclude non-English students, the General Chapter of 1261 took swift and decisive action, removing the provincial concerned and sending him to Germany for the remission of his sins. Not long after, the Germans were infected with the same virus: one wonders if the former English Provincial had actually been cured of his nationalism! There is always a strong sense that the Order's facilities anywhere in the world should be made available to any of the brethren who might benefit from them.

Study is not just about physical time and space, but about what we might call intellectual or spiritual time and space. It presupposes the freedom to think, to question, and to dispute. So the Order made its own the scholastic methods of lecturing, disputing and repeating. In class they read through classical texts again and again, especially the Bible. They discussed and debated controversial issues as they arose. They repeated to masters and other teachers what they were learning so that these permanent students would not only understand but be able to communicate their understanding to others.

The General Chapter held at Paris in 1236 instructed the friars to 'learn the language of those nearby', to learn the language of the neighbours, we might say:

> So we advise that, in all Provinces and convents, they (the friars) should learn the language of those nearby [*linguas addiscant illorum, qui sunt propinqui*][18].

---

17. Mulchahey, *First the Bow...*, page 133, with note 9
18. Fontana, *Constitutiones ...*, page 467, section 8.

This was required by the Order's missionary outreach, not only to Muslims and Jews in Spain, but also to other non-Latin speaking groups near and beyond the boundaries of Christendom. But we can also take it in a more general sense. The preacher must learn the language of the neighbours in the sense of understanding their lives, their concerns and their thoughts, their ways of finding meaning and seeking fulfilment. All of this must be studied too if the preacher is to serve the dialogue of salvation by preaching the Word that continues to become flesh in the hearts and lives of people. A letter about itinerancy (the friars' readiness to move) issued in 2003 by Carlos Azpiroz Costa, Master of the Order, includes a section on intellectual mobility, a readiness for fresh thinking and new challenges that has characterised the Order's great teachers in the past. It is enough to think of examples such as Francisco De Vitoria (1486-1546) and Henri Lacordaire (1802-1861).

Again, looking back along its tradition, it is clear that Dominican study, like Dominican government, is continually changing within a structure that remains. Some features are constantly present – the focus on preaching, the centrality of the study of Scripture, and (from the General Chapter of 1279 onwards) an endorsement of the reputation and teaching of Thomas Aquinas. These persist even as the Order has very different things to say about study from time to time and very different ways of organising it.

Differences arise through changing circumstances in the Order, in the Church and in the Church's engagement with the world. So, in the middle of the 13th century the questions posed by the new learning, especially the newly discovered thought of Aristotle, shape the agenda for Dominican thinking about study. Fresh challenges for the organisation of studies come as a result of the Black Death and the chaos that followed it, and from the great western schism when provinces were divided as to who the real Pope was.

The Reformation obliged the Order to strengthen its study of scripture, in particular of the biblical languages, and of Church history, if the friars were to engage in an intelligent and informed way in the controversies of that time. General Chapters began to refer more frequently to decisions of the Apostolic See and to 'the mind of the Church as it has come to be understood' (the Chapters of 1605 and 1656, for example). Convents were to have lectors in scripture, theology, and philosophy, the General Chapter of 1551 says, and smaller houses should have at least a lector in moral theology (to lead discussion of cases of conscience) and a lector in scripture. In 1670 the General Chapter decreed that cases of conscience should be discussed three times a week with the questions to be considered that week being announced on Sunday.

The questions of Dominican missionaries working in the New World stimulated fresh thought among the Dominican theologians of Salamanca particularly in relation to natural law and human rights. The rationalism of the 17th and 18th centuries made its mark too as the emphasis shifted to apologetics and to the defence of the faith where fresh questions from philosophy, history and science were emerging. General Chapters in those centuries began to speak more frequently of Thomist doctrines particularly those concerning grace and the freedom of the will. The Chapter of 1656 encouraged the brethren to 'avoid the itch of exotic doctrines that are not compatible with the authentic text of Saint Thomas'. The Chapter of 1725 urged them to study the text of Thomas itself and not just to read the commentators. 'Get into the river', it says, 'don't just stand on the banks'.[19]

FROM INSTRUMENTAL REASON TO REASON AS INTELLECT

Just as their predecessors in the Order were of their time, so Dominicans today have to think about these things in relation to the questions of our own time, the questions troubling the Order and the Church now. In this regard, it might not be completely fanciful to regard the change from Gillet (1930 - cf p. 109 above) to the Chapter held in River Forest (1968) – making their own once again the idea that study is an integral part of the Dominican form of religious life – as anticipating, or representing, a more general cultural shift in recent decades. Some talk about this as the crisis of modernity or as post-modernism. I want to mention briefly some of the difficulties it presents to Dominicans in thinking about study, as well as an opportunity that I believe it opens up for them.

---

19. ... *derelicto purissimo fonte quiescant in rivis* ...: Fontana, *Constitutiones* ..., page 254, section 4. See page 256, section 12 for the 'exotic itch'.

Intellectually, the time in which we are living is sceptical and relativist. In other words there is profound reserve, hesitation, and even disdain towards the idea that there is a truth to be discovered, a truth that human beings can communicate to each other and in relation to which they can come to have a common mind. Fergus Kerr, in a recent work, argues that there is now a variety of ways of interpreting Aquinas, and that some of these interpretations are simply 'incommensurable'.[20] In other words they cannot be brought into dialogue with each other and, it seems, neither ought they to be. We live with a variety of narratives established on the basis of a common, classical text, and there is something to be learned from thinking about each in turn.

We might say that one of the most important things we have learned from Aquinas is the need to engage with the best philosophy available in our time and to put it at the service of Christian theology. The difficulty today is in trying to determine where that best available philosophy is to be found. A recent summary by Stephen Priest, who teaches at Blackfriars, Oxford, says that philosophy since Kant can be divided (and not exhaustively!) into 'idealism, Marxism, pragmatism, existentialism, phenomenology, structuralism, Logical Positivism, linguistic analysis, post-structuralism, post-modernism'.[21] One of the great questions exercising the minds of Dominicans (and of the Church as a whole) in the past thirty years is the question of the philosophical resources to be drawn on in theology. General Chapters have been aware of this, as is everybody in the Order who teaches philosophy or theology.

The great intellectual controversy of the thirteenth century centred on the opening to philosophical study in the first place. Albert and Thomas, with the support of Humbert of Romans, led the Order and the Church in the work of translating and appropriating Aristotle. Older Dominicans regarded the whole enterprise with suspicion. When I was involved in drafting the *Ratio*

20. Fergus Kerr OP, *After Aquinas: Versions of Thomism* Blackwells, Oxford 2002

21. Stephen Priest, *The Oxford Companion to Philosophy, Second Edition*, Oxford University Press 2005, p. 172

Studiorum Particularis for the Province of Ireland, I was struck at how strongly some of the brethren believed that the Order has its own philosophy. They argued that this is more crucial in the formation of younger brethren than is a particular Dominican theology. A comparable conservative wisdom shared by 13th century and 20th century Dominicans led the first to be suspicious of any dealings with philosophy and the second to be suspicious of any dealings with philosophy that was not the philosophy of Aristotle and Aquinas!

This raises lots of questions, and the way forward has not yet been clearly seen. The question is fundamental, however, and of such profound interest to the Church as a whole, that in 1998 John Paul II devoted his encyclical letter *Fides et ratio* to it. It is not chauvinistic to claim that the Dominican tradition has something to say about all this, and Dominicans must continue to listen and speak together in various contexts in their efforts to understand better.

The contemporary cultural and intellectual situation also presents the Dominican tradition of study with an opportunity. The crisis of modernity which people call post-modernism has, at its heart, a loss of faith in the reach of reason. Reason, as it has been understood in modern times, has failed to arrive where it hoped to arrive, at universally accepted truth. Not only that, but many people believe that much damage has been done intellectually, and not only in the areas of moral philosophy and theology, by an understanding of reason that is purely instrumental and pragmatic.

Putting it a bit crudely could it be said that the Gillet understanding of the relationship of study to preaching was actually quite 'modernist'? People studied the theory of something for a few years and then got down to the practice of it. Knowledge unlocked the world and brought it, or at least part of it, under human control. Modern man was to be master of the universe and his power of reasoning was the great engine of this mastery. Professional people were trained in a discipline and could then be let loose – lawyers, doctors, teachers, preachers – to apply in practice what they had learned in theory.

To the extent that Dominicans understood their own study in this way they were, once again, people of their time, while sometimes failing to appreciate important elements of the specific tradition of which they are the heirs. What the River Forest (1968) decision makes possible is a recovery of the connection between study and contemplation, between study and a form of religious life. Of course properly scientific work is essential in whatever field they find themselves working, but for Dominicans the pursuit of knowledge has never been an end in itself. Rather do they seek wisdom in order to preach well, to speak to people words that are saving and healing. If we do live in post-modern times, then part of what people are seeking in this crisis of modernity is wisdom and not just knowledge, understanding and not just technical expertise. What I want to argue in the final part of this paper is that a spirituality of study is something of great value with which Dominicans are already familiar and which they are in a position to share with people today.

WISDOM BEYOND KNOWLEDGE

Thomas Aquinas recognised that the desire for knowledge is a passion in human beings that needs to be managed by a virtue that is part of temperance. All desires can get out of control, and the passion for knowledge is no exception. So he speaks of the virtue of *studiositas*, a moral virtue that the human being must acquire in order to be mature and in order to avoid vices that distort and unbalance the desire to know. Liam Walsh has written well about Thomas's account of this virtue[22].

The moral virtues themselves are moderated by prudence. Aquinas simply follows Aristotle in recognising that 'fact' and 'value', 'knowledge' and 'morality', cannot, in practice, be separated. Concretely, there is no morally neutral human act. Human endeavour is wise when it is in line with the requirements of prudence and when not in line with those requirements it is foolish. Prudence is a peculiarly human virtue needed because 'the

22 Liam Walsh OP, 'St Thomas and Study', in *La Formazione Integrale Domenicana al Servizio della Chiesa e della Società* (Edizioni Studio Domenicano, Bologna 1996) pages 223-52

human being as an originator of action is a union of desire and intellect', Aristotle says (*Nicomachean Ethics* VI.2). The person of good sense or practical wisdom has thoughts strengthened by appropriate desire and has desires focussed by correct thinking.

What Thomas says about prayer and contemplation is also relevant here. In a beautiful phrase he says that prayer is *desiderii interpres*, 'interpreter of desire' (*Summa theologiae* II.II 83, 1 *ad* 1). Prayer provides words for our desires. Contemplation is connected with truth and with language as we seek to understand the world, human destiny and God. Famously, Thomas speaks about a form of religious life that is centred on study and preaching and he defends it against its detractors (*ST* II.II 179-182, 187-188). Such a way of life is as close to perfection as is possible, he says, at least in its idea, for it involves not only the contemplation of truth for which human beings most deeply long but the communication to others of what has been contemplated.

It seems that people today are looking for precisely this kind of thing. Never before was so much knowledge available at the touch of buttons; but never before has so much knowledge been quite so superficial. Many people are unhappy with scientific expertise that operates in a moral vacuum, without reference to the implications, for the world, for human destiny, and for our relationship with God, of what is being done. People long for 'spirituality', an often unarticulated and uncertain quest. But the way in which wisdom has been understood in Dominican tradition, the different levels of wisdom, the respect for rational truth which yet recognises the need for supernatural light: all of this is to be found in the way they understand and pursue study. It could be made available to so many others if Dominicans were to succeed in making it genuinely a part of their own way of life, if they were to recover a strong and clear sense of themselves as student-preachers, living together in priory-schools, at the service of the Church and the world.

Let us summon two witnesses in support of this, neither of them Dominicans, but each a friend to the Dominicans. Each speaks about a need in the contemporary world for what study, as it is understood in the Dominican tradition, has to offer.

The first witness is Donald Nicholl, an English scholar and writer. The life of study, he says in an essay called 'The Beatitude of Truth', is a constant letting go and moving on as we come to realise, over and over, the inadequacy of what we have managed to say up to now. The famous scroll which Ezekiel is asked to eat (Ezekiel 3:1-3) and which Humbert of Romans recalls in his instruction to the brethren to 'eat the book'[23], tastes sweet at first. The adventure of finding things out, learning new things, coming to realise more deeply things we have known superficially, coming to understanding and insight: all of this is sweet and is the reward of study.

But, in the Book of Revelation, the scroll that is sweet on the lips and in the mouth turns bitter in the stomach (Revelation 10:8-11). The student, the one who is seeking truth, must be prepared always, says Donald Nicholl, for this bitterness, for the sadness of having to let go ideas and thoughts which he or she had come to cherish. There is 'a vein of sadness and tragedy which runs through all our efforts to know', he says. He is struck by the fact that Thomas Aquinas assigns to intellectuals and students the beatitude 'blessed are those who mourn' and he wonders why this should be:

> The answer Thomas gives is that, whenever our minds yearn towards some new truth, then we become afflicted with pain, because our whole being wishes to protect the balance of inertia and comfort which we have established for ourselves; and the pain is a symptom of our distress at its disturbance. Moreover, we experience a sort of bereavement when those formulations, images and symbols through which we had in the past appropriated truth have now to be abandoned. For those formulations, images and symbols have, over the years, become part of us. To lose them feels like losing part of ourselves. And we mourn that loss as we would the loss of a limb[24].

23 Humbert of Romans, *Treatise on Preaching*, paragraph 82 (Conlon translation, page 32; Tugwell translation, page 205). It provides the title for a recent article by Paul Murray OP, 'Eat the Book: Study in the Dominican Tradition', *Angelicum* 81 (2004) 405-30

24 Donald Nicholl, 'The Beatitude of Truth' in *The Beatitude of Truth* London 1997, pages 1-11, also published as 'The Search for Truth', *The Tablet*, 26 May 1990, pages 661-663. The quotation is from *The Beatitude of Truth*, pages 5-6.

The second witness to be summoned is the late Pope, John Paul II, who in 1994 had the following to say about what Dominicans can offer the Church and the world today:

> Your charism of studying the Word of God and human realities can be a powerful service today just as it was in the past. Fidelity to your charism requires from you an in-depth understanding of the cultural realities of the present, the prophetic denunciation of intellectual and moral deviations, and the inculturation of the faith. A Christian interpretation of the present cultural situation cannot fail to perceive its deep crisis, which is primarily one of reason. Many today are inclined to recognise only an instrumental role for reason, in relation to a scientific understanding of reality and to the technological application of its results, excluding the moral and transcendent dimensions from its competence. Consequently, man runs the risk of increasingly rejecting the role of reason as intellect ... [25]

He concludes by pointing us to Thomas Aquinas, to whom he had some years earlier given the title *doctor humanitatis*, and whom he holds up once again as a model, especially for Dominicans, of dialogue with the culture of our time.

We can bring together the testimony of these two witnesses. John Paul II invited the Dominicans to appreciate anew the positive theology that is part of their tradition and that equips them to encourage and value science, philosophy, and learning generally. Donald Nicholl invited them to appreciate anew the negative theology that is also part of their tradition, not only in figures like Eckhart and Catherine of Siena, but in the Order's greatest theological mind, Thomas Aquinas. That negative theology, as Paul Murray puts it, 'frees us from the tyranny of a single vision'.[26]

For Dominicans wisdom is as close and as ordinary as the child beginning to learn how to read and write. But it is also the hard-won insight of the philosopher and the hard-won experience of the parent or teacher. The Order that seeks to preach the Word or

25 John Paul II, 'Kindle the Torch of Christian Proclamation', in *La Formazione Integrale Domenicana al Servizio della Chiesa e della Società* Edizioni Studio Domenicano, Bologna 1996, pages 433-44. The quotation is from pages 441-42.
26 Murray, 'Eat the Book', page 424.

Wisdom of God must itself be a place where the quest for wisdom is supported and encouraged. This is not only about study and academic work. It is not only about prayer and contemplation. It is about a way of life that combines these two, the hard work of study and the hard work of prayer. Simon Tugwell notes that ideally, for the early Dominicans, study and prayer merged to form a whole life of attentiveness to God and to his words and works, a combination which William of Tocco sees achieved in the life of Thomas Aquinas[27].

This way of life involves letting go and moving on, intellectually as well as in other ways, but the mourning which accompanies this is, we are told, a blessing. For it prepares those who pursue it for a wisdom not won through human effort but given as a gift of the Spirit. On more than one occasion, quoting Dionysius the Areopagite, Thomas Aquinas says that Christians who persevere 'not only learn about divine things, but come to experience them' (*non solum discens sed et patiens divina*). Most significantly he quotes this saying in the opening question of the *Summa* and in his account of the Holy Spirit's gift of wisdom (*ST* I 1; II.II 45). There is a knowledge of God, he says, that is learned through study and there is a knowledge of God that is connatural with its object and in which the one who knows has become attuned to God. This highest wisdom is the gift that accompanies charity and enables the one who loves to know the deepest things about the object of his love.

Our *studium*, as said at the outset, is our desire and passion, that which excites and attracts us, the thing that wins our love. When our passion is for God, for speaking with God or of God, then we must be prepared for bitterness and for sweetness, for a mourning that is deep like God's compassion, and a joy that is eternal like Wisdom's delight in the presence of the Heavenly Father[28].

27 William of Tocco, *Life of St Thomas Aquinas*, paragraph 30, as cited by Tugwell in *Early Dominicans*, page 107, with note 27

28 See Vivian Boland OP, '*Non solum discens sed et patiens divina*. The Wanderings of an Aristotelian Fragment', *Roma, magistra mundi. Itineraria culturae medievalis*. Mélanges offerts au Père L.E.Boyle à l'occasion de son 75e anniversaire édités par J.Hamesse, Fédération Internationale des Instituts d'Études Médiévales, Textes et études du moyen âge X, Louvain-la-Neuve, 1998, volume I, pages 55-69 and Donagh O'Shea OP, 'Meister Eckhart on the Road to Damascus', in the present volume (pp 97-106).

VIII

Preaching: The Art and Craft

JAMES DONLEAVY, OP

PREACHING: THE ART AND CRAFT

James Donleavy, OP

Humpty Dumpty's tone was rather scornful: 'When I use a word, it means just what I choose it to mean – neither more or less'. 'The question is', said Alice, 'whether you can make things mean different things'. 'The question is', said Humpty Dumpty, 'which is to be master – that's all'.[1] Humpty Dumpty's linguistic philosophy will make brief appearances throughout this chapter, but it is sufficient to state, with Humpty Dumpty's authority, 'the art' means what you say in preaching and 'the craft' is how that message is communicated. However, the two are going to overlap for I cut my sociological teeth in the days when Marshall McLuhan was the guru and the current slogan was 'the medium is the message' – or as the great Irish Dominican preacher and publicist, Gabriel Harty, insisted, 'the sizzle sells the sausage'.

GO AND PREACH TO ALL NATIONS [2] – PRAY ALWAYS [3]

Preaching is at the centre of Dominican life. Whether we are speaking about the art or the craft, we are talking about a formative and an empowering force that we call the Dominican way of life. How deeply this life is lived in an individual, or priory, or province, is judged by the enthusiasm and zeal, commitment and dedication to the Order's original charism. St Dominic founded the Order on the highest ideals. 'A life of teaching and preaching deriving from a fullness of contemplation is to be preferred to contemplation on its own: to share what one contemplates with others is better than merely to contemplate it oneself'.[4]

According to Edward Schillebeeckx, OP, the renewal represented by the foundation of his Order by Dominic lay in the combination

---

1. Lewis Carroll, *Through the Looking Glass*, Folio Society, London, 1962, p.75
2. Mark 16:16
3. 1 Thessalonians 5:17
4. Thomas Aquinas, *Summa theologiae*, edited and translated by Timothy McDermott, Eyre and Spottiswoode, 1989, p.465

of a contemplative religious life and a priestly orientation on preaching (a notion he took over directly from Clerissac[5]). In his view, the 'tension' that emerged here 'between the essentially contemplative focus of the religious life and the apostolic attitude of the Order, gives Dominican spirituality its core instinct'.[6] In a simpler and personal way, I have constantly struggled with the call of the diocesan priesthood and the attractiveness of the Cistercian way of life. It is from this spirituality that our preaching springs.

THE CHALLENGE OF PREACHING TODAY

Preaching has always been difficult, and each age is faced with its own particular problems. However, with a certain indulgent insularity, we think that today the problems are greater than at any previous time. Maybe we are correct in that opinion. Consciously and unconsciously the way of verbal/visual communication has radically changed in the last thirty years. This, in no small way, is the result of the ubiquity of television.

We now live in a culture that can be characterised as the '3-minute' culture – the culture of the short attention span, where politicians no longer address us in speeches, but in 30-second 'sound bites' and through 'photo opportunities'; a world in which the news comes to us in 90-second bits, each disconnected from the last, in a plethora of little stories and images; where we are so used to the fast editing of adverts and pop promos that the traditional Hollywood film seems so slow as to be almost quaint. It is a culture which induces us to graze the TV channels, zapping back and forth whenever our boredom threshold is triggered, rather than watching a programme. It is a culture where very rarely does anyone do just one thing at a time, in a concentrated way for an extended period; it is increasingly a culture catering for people with the attention span of a flea. So look at the media: narrative is replaced by flow; connection replaced by disconnection; sequence by randomness. The cost is memory. We are increasingly an 'amnesiac culture', where everything is jumbled up together in an over-polluted swamp of images and sensations – a kind of fast food culture for

5. Eric Borgman, *Edward Schillebeeckx*, Continuum, London, 2003, p.118
6. *ibid.*

the mind, served up in easy-to-chew, bite-sized sections, where everyone snacks all the time, but no one (hardly) ever consumes the intellectual equivalent of a square meal[7].

There is, I find, a marked difference in the receptivity of people in their 40s and upwards compared with the younger generations. The older group 'did' their catechism which was also the theological model followed in many seminaries. Hence some members of the congregation may have some (atavistic) folk memory of certain words and phrases which are just gobbledygook to others. A priest describing the death of a 17 year-old said 'when I called to the house I felt that the prayers and words I had to offer were totally alien to these fine young people. I felt a stranger in their midst'.[8]

Back to Humpty Dumpty. Words are the building blocks, though not the only ones, of the preacher's craft. Words need to be fresh, creative, forceful, and beautiful. Luke tells us that the people of Nazareth were enchanted by the gracious words that came from his (Jesus') lips[9]. Some preachers make the mistake of presuming that because they speak English (and I am sure it holds true for all languages), and, once they have ideas in their heads, there is an automatic conjunction between word and idea, that – hey presto – out pops an articulate, understandable, attractive expression. Alas! It is not always so.

The emptiness of the words of many preachers was never perhaps better caught than by George Orwell, sixty years ago in his *Politics and the English Language*: when one watches some tired hack on the platform mechanically repeating the familiar phrases – 'free people of the world, stand shoulder to shoulder' – one often has the curious feeling that one is not watching a live human being but some kind of dummy: a feeling which suddenly becomes stronger at moments when the light catches the speaker's spectacles and turns them into blank discs which seem to have no eyes behind them.

7. James Curran et al., editors, *Cultural Studies and Communications*, Arnold, London 1996, p.61

8. Des Byrne CSSp, *The Furrow*, April 2005, p.248

9. Luke 4:22

Mutatis mutandis, I fear this could be applied to many a preacher. To add insult to injury, we might add Senator William McAdoo's famous attack on President Warren Harding: his speeches leave the impression of an army of pompous phrases moving over the landscape in search of an idea. Sometimes these meandering words would actually capture a straggling thought and bear it triumphantly, a prisoner in their midst, until it died of servitude and overwork[10].

PREACHING – SCHEMATIC OR CONTEXTUAL?

While preaching was never considered either one or the other of these in hermetically sealed compartments, yet there was a tendency to look on 'the ordinary homily' as instruction. A topic of instruction was posted at the back of the church for every Sunday and was meticulously followed. The context did not seem particularly important. It was the same with theology.

When I studied theology formally (at the end of the 50s and in the early 60s) I had grown up listening to my father telling of the hell of four years in the trenches during the Great War (1914-1918). I had spent nights in air-raid shelters as the German bombers were wreaking havoc on the city of Liverpool. All those in the class could remember the Nagasaki and Hiroshima explosions, and the discovery of the Holocaust. Yet these were never mentioned in theology for it seemed that God could be controlled with our sophisticated metaphysical jargon. God did not seem to have any connection with the world's experience.

It may seem a little simplistic, but for me that debate ended with the publication of *Gaudium et Spes.* We could appreciate St Dominic's method of preaching and the reason he loved the Gospel according to St Matthew. 'The saint (Dominic) was not abstract in his language, nor were his words remote from the sentiments of his hearers. He felt keenly the hopes and trials of this agricultural population which at the time was suffering from the effects of a persistent drought'.[11]

10. John Humphries, *Lost for Words,* Hodder and Stoughton, London, 2004, p.186 – a must for all speakers.

11. M.-H.Vicaire OP, *St Dominic and His Times,* Darton, Longman and Todd, London, 1964, p.255

Learn from Mr Mammon! The American motor industry produces good cars and therefore people should buy them. The Japanese start with the customer and answers his or her motoring needs. The Japanese sell more cars than the Americans do. The French think they are the only people who know about wine and should have the lion's share of the market. The Australians have done much research into people's palates and tastes, and are now overtaking the French in selling wine. There is a lesson here for preachers if we can read the signs.

I do not write for eternity, but for the men and women of today who are in a particular historical situation. I try to respond to their questions. So my theology has a date; it is contextual, but at the same time I want to go beyond the situation. That is the aim of my works because I try to take into account the questions of all men and women[12].

Preaching is not about propounding a theoretical or cerebral series of doctrines but knowing people's fears and hopes and disappointments and helping them to cope with their situation by bringing good news and the power of Jesus Christ. As we say in modern terms, it is knowing 'where people are at' and speaking there. Our sermons need far more instances of 'e.g.' than 'i.e.'.

PREACHING AS A CRAFT

Preaching is a practical skill, and the question has to be asked: what can we do so as to ensure a vision for the next 150 years? For the Province of Ireland, a school of preaching could be established from the resources and talents available. Friars (and lay people) would be encouraged, cajoled and expected to avail themselves of this facility. An on-going course of formation could be organised to help and instruct the friars in the creativity and expertise needed in presenting the Word today.

For communities of the Irish Province, preaching needs to be regarded as a corporate, community act and not an individual occupation. There has been a ridiculous custom in the Province that we do not listen to each other's preaching. Can you imagine playing golf with a companion (those who do play golf) and asking

12. Borgman, op.cit., p.5

him not to look at you as you strike the ball because you might be doing something less than perfect and you do not want to be told?! We need to talk about our preaching and sermons. Wonderful books have been published recently that would be of enormous help to the preacher. Our libraries should be kept up-to-date and new books discussed.

For individuals of the Irish Province, it is essential to pray always before and after preaching. It is essential to prepare well – it is very obvious when a preacher is 'treading water'. It is essential to keep reading – a book a month, a magazine each month. It is helpful to ask a few informed and interested lay people to listen to you preaching and to give a critical appraisal afterwards. Heed what they say. And practise, practise, practise.

In every sermon the preacher tries, in the words of St Augustine, to teach, to please, and to urge. But the preacher does more! He or she is there to help people dream – not that they fall asleep during a sermon (though that is not necessarily a bad thing to do!) – but to help people see what can be in their lives, in all our lives, with the power of the Spirit of Jesus. The preacher is there to inspire hope. 'Good represents the reality of which God is the dream'.[13]

The Chief Rabbi of Great Britain, Dr Jonathan Sachs, writes:

> ... but I have learned this: that each of us is here for a purpose; that discerning that purpose takes time and honesty, knowledge of ourselves and knowledge of the world, but it is there to be discovered. Each of us has a constellation of gifts, an unreplicated radius of influence, be it as small as a family or as large as a state, we can be a transformative presence; and if we listen carefully enough we will hear the voice of God in the human heart telling us that there is work to do and he needs us[14].

As people ponder a sermon in their hearts may they say: 'now I have a dream'.

---

13. Iris Murdoch, *Metaphysics as a Guide to Morals*, Chatto and Windus, London, 1992, p.496

14. Jonathan Sachs, *To Heal a Fractured World*, Continuum, London, 2005, p.272

IX

The Homily:
Serving, not Dominating

PHILIP GLEESON, OP

THE HOMILY:
SERVING, NOT DOMINATING

Philip Gleeson, OP

In 1963 the Second Vatican Council produced the Constitution on the Sacred Liturgy *(Sacrosanctum concilium)*. In the section on the Mass it said (n° 52):

By means of the homily, the mysteries of the faith and the guiding principles of the Christian life are expounded from the sacred text during the course of the liturgical year. The homily is strongly recommended, since it forms part of the liturgy itself[1].

Since then the homily has figured in several official documents, including the Code of Canon Law of 1983 (canon 767), which says it is 'the most important form of preaching'. It is given ample treatment in Chupungco[2] and in Sartore and Triacca[3].

Without going over everything contained in the manuals and encyclopedias, this article emphasises that the documents present the homily as part of a liturgical celebration. It looks at some of the characteristics of the homily that are listed in the documents, and at some of the questions that may be raised.

The idea that the eucharistic prayer is the high point of the Mass is fairly familiar. Perhaps less familiar is the idea that it is the reading of the gospel that is the high point of the liturgy of the word (Introduction to the Lectionary, 1981, n° 13; General Instruction of the Roman Missal, 2005, n° 60). Alleluia, procession, candles, incense, all help to focus attention on the reading of the gospel.

---

1. Austin Flannery, OP (general editor), *The Basic Sixteen Documents of Vatican II: Constitutions, Decrees, Declarations*. A Completely Revised Translation in Inclusive Language, 1996, Northport, New York, Costello Publishing Company / Dublin, Dominican Publications, p.136

2. Anscar J. Chupungco, OSB (editor), *Handbook for Liturgical Studies: Volume III: The Eucharist*, 1999, Collegeville, The Liturgical Press, pp. 189-208

3. Domenico Sartore & Achille M. Triacca (editors), *Dictionnaire encyclopédique de la liturgie, Adaptation française sous la direction d'Henri Delhougne*, Vol. I, A-L, 1992, Tournai, Brepols, pp. 560-575.

Down through the ages the congregation has stood for the gospel in Latin whether it was sung or said. The homilist needs to be conscious of the way in which the ritual rises to a crest just before the homily. This realisation is necessary if the homily is to be properly placed in relation to the whole of the Mass. The homily follows on the gospel not just by coming after it. It is generated by the gospel, flows from the gospel, welcomes and prolongs the gospel. (Occasionally it may draw on other Scripture texts, and even other liturgical texts or rites, all of course incorporating the good news in one way or another.)

Following the lead of the *Constitution on the Liturgy* (n° 35), the Introduction to the Lectionary says (n° 24):

> The purpose of the homily at Mass is that the spoken word of God and the liturgy of the eucharist may together become 'a proclamation of God's wonderful works in the history of salvation, the mystery of Christ.'

Further on, while dealing with the function of the one presiding, the Introduction to the Lectionary (n° 41) has this to say:

> The one presiding exercises his proper office and the ministry of the word of God also as he preaches the homily. In this way he leads his brothers and sisters to an affective knowledge of holy Scripture. He opens their souls to gratitude for the wonderful works of God. He strengthens their faith in the word that in the celebration becomes a sacrament through the Holy Spirit. Finally he prepares them for a fruitful reception of communion and invites them to embrace the demands of the Christian life.

'An affective knowledge of holy Scripture' is the first aim that is listed. There is no scarcity of reminders that the homily should be based on Scripture, and should stem from a loving appreciation of the Scriptures. But here the lectionary suggests that there is a sense in which the homily points towards Scripture, and should help people to love and appreciate Scripture. It does not simply get things out of the Scriptures, but gets people into the Scriptures. In one way or another it treats the Bible as the Good Book, and invites the congregation to savour this Good Book. A homily that helps the congregation to appreciate the Bible is performing a valuable service to the Church, even if it does not manage to draw practical conclusions.

'Gratitude for the wonderful works of God' is the second aim given in the list. Thanksgiving for the wonderful things that God has done is one of the great themes of the Bible. It is a major part of the eucharistic prayer. In fostering a spirit of thanksgiving, the homily enters into the spirit of the Bible, and prepares the assembly for the liturgy of the eucharist. Thanksgiving permeates the whole celebration, and the homily needs to be in tune with this.

'Strengthens their faith in the word that in the celebration becomes a sacrament through the Holy Spirit.' The Lectionary speaks of the word becoming a sacrament through the Holy Spirit, a sign and a source of the new life of faith. One is reminded of the parallel drawn by Vatican II's *Dei verbum*, the Dogmatic Constitution on Divine Revelation (n° 21):

> The church has always venerated the divine Scriptures as it has venerated the Body of the Lord, in that it never ceases, above all in the sacred liturgy, to partake of the bread of life and to offer it to the faithful from the one table of the word of God and the Body of Christ.

One is reminded also of the more cautious statement in the Introduction to the Lectionary (n° 10):

> The church has honoured the word of God and the eucharistic mystery with the same reverence, although not with the same worship, and has always and everywhere intended and endorsed such honour. [...] The church is nourished spiritually at the table of God's word and at the table of the eucharist; from the one it grows in wisdom and from the other in holiness.

Whatever about the subtleties of such statements, the homily is meant to support and strengthen the response of faith to the word of God proclaimed in the gospel and other readings. This response is imagined as an eating at the table of the word. Eating involves activity on the part of the eater. The response of the assembly (including the homilist) to the word is like tasting, enjoying, swallowing and digesting. At the beginning of one of his sermons (Sermon 95,1) Augustine says:

When I expound the holy Scriptures to you, it is as though I
were breaking bread to you. For your part, receive it hungrily,
and belch out a fat praise from your hearts; and those of you
who are rich enough to keep excellent tables, don't be mean
and lean with your works and good deeds. So what I am
dishing out to you is not mine. What you eat, I eat; what you
live on, I live on. We share a common larder in heaven; that,
you see, is where the word of God comes from[4].

This quotation, besides reminding us that table manners differ
from culture to culture, shows how vividly Augustine grasped the
image of the eating of the word, an eating which is active, and
which should be accompanied by sharing with others.

'Preparation for communion' is another aim of the homily, and,
very closely linked with this, 'invitation to embrace the demands
of the Christian life'. The lectionary is suggesting a movement from
Scripture, through the homily, into communion, and out into the
living of life. This is also found earlier in the Introduction to the
Lectionary (n° 24):

[The homily] must always lead the community of the faithful
to celebrate the eucharist wholeheartedly, 'so that they may
hold fast in their lives to what they have grasped by their
faith'.

Exhortation is an element of the homily, but not the only element.
And these texts suggest that instead of going directly to exhortation,
the homily should take the path so often suggested by the
postcommunion prayers. The life to which we are invited is the
life which is celebrated in the eucharist. The love to which the
assembly is called is the love celebrated in the eucharist. In the
context of the Mass, the homily does not simply invite people to be
good, but to 'live the Mass'. Of course this does not mean that every
homily must explicitly mention communion and the living out of
communion. If the homily is centred on Christ, present throughout
the whole of the Mass, it will prepare for communion and give
encouragement towards Christian living.

---

4. *The Works of Saint Augustine.* III/4: *Sermons 94A-147A.* Translation and
Notes, Edmund Hill, OP, 1992, Brooklyn, New York, New City Press, p. 24.

It has been noted that the official texts say that the eucharistic prayer is the high point of the whole celebration, and that the reading of the gospel is the high point of the liturgy of the word. Sometimes this is questioned. It has been argued that the communion is the climax of the Mass, whether meal or sacrifice is emphasised[5]. Similarly, it could be argued that it is the congregation's assimilation of the word that is the climax of the liturgy of the word. But perhaps there is no pressing need to decide exactly where the highest points are. What matters is that the different parts are related to each other, and that there is a movement through the Mass towards communion. The homily should be part of the movement, not isolated from it or even going against it.

It is surely in the light of these texts, which see the homily as a part of the movement that runs through the Mass, that the familiar theme of the catechetical value of the liturgy should be understood. The Catechism of the Catholic Church (n° 1074) calls the liturgy 'the privileged place for catechising the People of God'. Of course not all catechesis can be done during the liturgy. But catechesis should never become separated from the liturgical life of the Church, and the liturgy itself, including the homily that is part of the liturgy, is one of the best ways in which the message is communicated. What is true of all liturgy is especially true of the Mass, which communicates the mystery into which we are called.

It is easy enough to paint this picture of a homily which fits beautifully into the Mass. Everyone knows that the reality is difficult to achieve. There are the limitations of the individual homilist. There are also the limitations arising from a particular situation. What should be done if in fact the homily is the only ministry of the word for many people? How should the desired involvement of the community in preparation and follow-up be organised?

There are problems on other levels too. The question of the distinction between the ordained and the non-ordained is not the least of these. While granting that people who have not been ordained to preach may in fact preach, and may sometimes even

---

5. David N. Power, OMI, *The Eucharistic Mystery: Revitalizing the Tradition,* 1992, Dublin, Gill and Macmillan, pp. 292-293. Power quotes Von Balthasar.

give a liturgical homily outside the eucharistic celebration itself (*Instruction on Certain Questions regarding the Collaboration of the Non-ordained Faithful in the Sacred Ministry of the Priest*, 1997, Article 3, §4), the texts exclude the non-ordained from giving the homily during Mass. Normally the presiding bishop or priest gives the homily. It may however be given by other concelebrating bishops or priests, by bishops or priests who are not concelebrating, and, from time to time, by deacons. But on no account may a layperson give it. The texts recognise that a layperson may have theological competence and communication skills. They clearly imply that a layperson may be well capable of producing something that could be mistaken for a homily. *Redemptionis sacramentum*, 2004, n° 74, notes that if a layperson is to speak at Mass, it should be after the postcommunion. The texts are anxious to draw a very definite line between ordained and non-ordained. Whatever about the rights and wrongs of the particular question, these texts show an awareness of how powerfully the liturgy operates as a way of excluding or including, and a way of positioning people in relation to each other in the community.

It is an old question. The Scripture scholars have told us much about prophets and teachers, about speaking out or remaining silent in the assembly. The question was known to Eusebius (*Ecclesiastical History*, Bk 6, Ch. 19), who describes an argument about whether it was right to allow Origen, while still a layman, to preach in the presence of the bishop (presumably in the Sunday assembly). In favour of the practice was Alexander, bishop of Jerusalem, and Theoctistus, bishop of Caesarea. Strongly against it was Origen's own bishop, Demetrius of Alexandria. Alexander and Theoctistus maintained that the practice was fairly widespread, and acceptable because done under the auspices of the bishop. Demetrius protested that it was unheard of. Perhaps the argument is a sign that a transition to a stricter regime was under way. Of interest too is what Jerome wrote in his letter to Nepotian (Letter 52, 7), where he grumbles about those bishops who refuse to let presbyters preach in their presence, either because of jealousy or impatience. It was a letter that, for many reasons, irritated many of Jerome's contemporaries.

If the debate about who may give the homily at Mass is allowed to develop, it inevitably spills over into the debate about who should be ordained. The question may be asked: if a person has the gifts needed to preach the homily, why not ordain that person deacon or priest? And there is the related question of whether the sacrament of orders is open to the kind of development that Karl Rahner wondered about thirty years ago[6], a development into more variations and subdivisions within the sacrament of orders. As tends to emerge in most liturgical discussions, the real discussion is about the Church and the way in which people are related to each other in the Church.

There is another difficulty that is just touched on in the Introduction to the Lectionary. In justifying the omission of certain texts from the lectionary, n° 77 notes that some biblical passages are pastorally unsuitable for liturgical reading, and that they present real difficulties. These texts seem to become more rather than less difficult as time goes on. Gloating over fallen enemies, writing off those who no longer walk with us, using 'Jews' in a derogatory sense, assuming that patriarchy is all right, condoning slavery, any or all of these can make it hard to say, 'This is the word of the Lord' or 'This is the Gospel of the Lord'. Catherine Hilkert has written a thoughtful and informative chapter entitled, 'Trust the Text or Preach the Gospel?'[7] No one can accuse her of giving simplistic answers, and it would be hard to disagree with the suggestion (in which Hilkert agrees with Sandra Schneiders) that certain texts should not be read unless the preacher is prepared to preach against the text in the name of the Gospel. And there can be no doubting the rightness of what she says about the importance of the community's role in discerning how to wrestle with such texts.

Whatever about the need to be nuanced about the way in which the reading of Scripture is the word of the Lord, a sacrament in some sense, it would certainly be unreal and dangerous to present the homily simply as part of a great downward sweep, coming from God through Christ in the Church and issuing forth from the

---

6. *Theological Investigations*, XIV, 1976, pp. 209-210

7. Mary Catherine Hilkert, *Naming Grace: Preaching and the Sacramental Imagination*, 1998, New York, Continuum, pp. 71-88.

mouth of the preacher. We would think it very presumptuous for the homilist to conclude with, 'This is the word of the Lord'! This is not to say that the preacher abandons all hope of teaching or of leading into the mystery, nor that there is no need for prophecy, for speaking out in God's name. But the preacher needs to be a listener and a searcher as much as a speaker. The homilist is not a dietician regulating the diet of the congregation, but a fellow connoisseur of the wonderful fare on offer.

All good preaching is aware of its limitations. And no matter how good a homily is, every homily is bound to be overshadowed by what is to follow. No homily can compare with the body given and the blood shed. No homily should try to compare with them. Homilies are worse than useless if they do not humbly serve the celebration of which they are a part. As the Lutheran theologian, Wolfhart Pannenberg, has written:

> Every celebration of the Eucharist reenacts the reality that constitutes the foundation of the church, and that happens not only in the sense of memorial but also in the symbolic power of the Eucharist, where the essence of the church itself is alive, present, and effective. Lest I be unclear on this point, let me put it more bluntly: The Eucharist, not the sermon, is in the center of the church's life. The religious individuality that produces itself in the pulpit, while telling us that it is really the word of God that we hear, should not be the center of worship. The sermon should serve, not dominate, in the church. It should serve the presence of Christ which we celebrate in the Eucharist[8].

8. Wolfhart Pannenberg, *Christian Spirituality and Sacramental Community*. (Darton, Longman and Todd, London 1984), p. 40.

X

Preaching the Word in Situations of Distress and Alienation

BENEDICT HEGARTY, OP

PREACHING THE WORD IN SITUATIONS OF DISTRESS AND ALIENATION

Benedict Hegarty, OP

Times of distress and alienation can be rough moments for a preacher, intent on communication. The most common encounters with distress are in times of bereavement or illness. In bereavement there is the numbness of grief. There is the appalling experience of loss, the sense of emptiness. Bereavement can set one at sea in currents of doubt, question, bewilderment and loss. Over fifteen hundred years ago when Augustine described the death of a friend, he spoke for all of us. 'My heart was black with grief. Whatever I looked upon had the air of death. The things we had done together became sheer torment without him. My eyes were restless looking for him, but he was not there. I hated all places because he was not in them. They could not say 'He will soon come', as they would in his life when he was absent'.[1]

Severe suffering is often if not usually accompanied by feelings of abandonment by God and a sense of isolation from one's own community. This sense of isolation is touched on when C.S.Lewis's wife spoke to him on her deathbed. 'Even if we both died at exactly the same moment, as we lie here side by side, it would be just as much a separation as the one you are afraid of. Alone into the alone'.[2] There is nothing soothing one can say to a patient who has just learnt bad news and is traumatised by the collapse of whatever sense of power and control they thought they possessed. Parents and relatives faced with the serious illness of a child have no time for the anodynes of comforting words. All they can think of is the peril of their loved one.

The issue of alienation is different from that of distress. Alienation conveys a more directed response to the preacher's mission. It positively rejects it as irrelevant and distasteful, out of

---

1 Augustine, *Confessions* Book 4, chapter 4
2 C.S. Lewis, *A Grief Observed*, 1961, New York, Bantam Books, pp.14-15

touch, intrusive to the subject's life situation. It can create its own culture, which is against everything the preacher stands for. It can shape words, thoughts, actions and values. It generates a situation in which parties cannot hear the same message, live by the same values, or support the same cultural paradigms.

While different forms of alienation can be seen across the conscious world, it achieves a particular refinement in human society. Alienation can work out a well-developed system to support itself, giving it a coherence and plausibility that gives a deadly intensity to division, religious conflict and war.

One of the problems of human communication is the bewildering variety of conviction. Long ago Pascal captured the issue in his famous statement that what is true on one side of the Pyrenees is false on the other. On the positive side this brings a rich variety to human experience and wisdom; yet, all the same, cultures can reinforce alienation between peoples and nations. As human beings we have no species-specific environment. We can live in deserts or in fields; in the tropics or the Arctic; on land or at sea, and now in space. There are quite a number of ways of being human depending on the different social, physical, and climatic situations in which we find ourselves. In all these situations we create our understanding of ourselves, weaving webs of meaning that support us. These patterns of everyday life are sustained by individuals in relationship with one another. This is done by language, acts, symbolic gestures, and so on. Within this comforting context the individual feels at home. The discomfort of decision-making is reduced. What is right is the received wisdom created by individuals who have gone before us. To depart from the created cultural patterns is to feel disorientated as an individual and to be branded as either eccentric (if harmless) or dangerous (if seen by the community as *too* different).

As far as the preacher is concerned, alienation can have its roots in a variety of causes. Cultural change has removed the structures that gave plausibility to regular, unquestioned religious practice. Alienation can have its roots in personal hurts and upsets reaching back years. The experience of the Church's lack of penitence, humility and transparency has angered many. Preachers can seem out of touch with people's struggles; and their priggish certainties do not commend their message. Sermons can seem incoherent, badly prepared, and foolish. Liturgies can be experienced as dull and unimaginative. When we look at life at a little greater depth, perhaps the situation is not quite so bleak as it seems. Is there an abyss of difference so deep that no bridge can cross it? Is there a structure, roadmap, or understanding of human life in which the preacher can place himself vis-à-vis the other person and that can be seen as a starting point in the relationship between both of them? Not too great a gulf separates the preacher from the distressed and alienated. Tapping into our shared humanity is the preacher's greatest asset. We have all walked dark roads. Human experience tells the story of a shared and common humanity that enables men and women to recover from conflict, shake off the paradigms that supported division, and live in a peace that would be quite foreign to a previous generation. Indeed the ability to make peace, to reach across apparently unbridgeable chasms of difference and establish new relationships, is wonderfully human.

Centuries of reflection have noted the open-ended quality of human life. Neither the distressed nor the alienated, not even the preacher, is caught in a time frame. All three are on the same journey. All three are thirsting, seeking, questioning, and searching. It is part of what it is to be a human being. Pathways may differ, and the answers may drive apart or set at odds, but the questions unite. Communication is difficult but there is a comforting *entente* in the fellowship of the journey. This means that people are never completely alienated from one another. They are united in the questions if not in the answers.

This sense of journeying has been reflected on in many theological contexts. A brief glimpse of the Biblical treatment is called for. Then we will look at it from the point of view of four deep thinkers, widely separated by time or faith or culture.

The Bible opens with the words 'in the beginning God created the heavens and the earth', Genesis 1:1. The Book of Revelation, and with it the Christian body of sacred literature, ends with a note of longing and triumph: 'I am coming soon. I am the Alpha and the Omega, the first and the last, the beginning and the end. I am the root and the offspring of David, the bright morning star. Come ... I am coming soon', Revelation 22:13-20. As God is seen at the beginning of all creation, at the opening of this literature, so now he is seen at the end, drawing the whole cosmic adventure to a conclusion.

In the Biblical understanding, this working out of God's purposes from the beginning of time to the end is seen in the processes of human history. Time and history, therefore, in their beginning and their consummation are of supreme importance in the Biblical tradition where life is seen to derive its meaning not only from its origin but also from its goal which beckons it forward and upward. We are on a journey; and pilgrims are full of questions, always searching. They have not put down roots. They are looking for a hopeful future. In Christian terms, this search finds classical expression in the words of Augustine, 'you made us for you and our hearts are restless until they rest in you'.[3]

THOMAS AQUINAS

Many years ago, in the pre-Vatican II days, when Tallaght Priory was a centre of enlightened Thomistic culture, we learned that in the Middle Ages, Thomas Aquinas wrote of a natural desire for God which springs from the natural desire of the mind for knowledge and the natural desire of the will for happiness. This insight is situated in a broader vision of the teleological character of nature, that directedness towards its own growth and fulfilment with which God endows every creature as a permanent intrinsic principle of movement flowing naturally from it[4]. Mind is made for truth[5]. The will is made for love. It is natural for the human mind to seek explanations so that when it apprehends that creation is an effect, it inevitably seeks its cause[6]. The human mind naturally seeks the understanding of God[7]. It is equally natural for the human

---

3 Augustine, *Confessions* Book 1, chapter 1: *Tu nos fecisti ad te, et cor nostrum inquietum est donec requiescat in te.*

4 Thomas Aquinas, *Summa theologiae* I 103,1 *ad* 3

5 Thomas Aquinas, *op. cit.*, I.II 3,7

6 Thomas Aquinas, *op. cit.*, I 12,1: *Inest enim homini naturale desiderium cognoscendi causam, cum intuetur effectum; et ex hoc admiratio in hominibus consurgit,* 'there is in the human being a natural desire, on identifying an effect, to know the cause; it is from this that wonder arises in human beings'.

7 Thomas Aquinas, *op. cit.*, I.II 94, 2: *Homo habet naturalem inclinationem ad hoc quod veritatem cognoscat de Deo,* 'the human being has a natural inclination towards knowing the truth about God'.

will to seek the complete fulfilment of desire in the *summum bonum*, the 'highest good' in which all created good participates[8]. In the reaching of the mind and of the will for any objective, there is an implicit reaching for God[9]. According to Aquinas the reach for the future and transcendence are embedded in our being.

KARL RAHNER

Long after St Thomas Aquinas, the highly influential 20th century Roman Catholic theologian Karl Rahner argued for a transcendental openness to being as such, as the *a priori* possibility of having any knowledge of the infinite. It is very like what Aquinas was teaching. At one level a person is a product of a series of empirical causes, social, historical, and so on. Yet we experience ourselves in our subjectivity as the product of what is radically foreign to all this. In our subjectivity and questioning we see ourselves as greater than the sum of our causes. A finite system is directed to a finite operation, whereas we human beings are not tied to a definite operation or to one single or definite cause. We have an infinite horizon of questioning. As Rahner puts it: 'The infinite horizon of human questioning is experienced as an horizon which recedes further and further the more answers man can discover'.[10] The human person can try to evade the mysterious infinite that opens up before us in our questions. Out of fear of the mysterious we can take flight to the familiar and the everyday and try to forget it. But this is not possible because the infinite to which we experience ourselves exposed permeates our everyday activities. We are always on a journey. None of the goals we achieve in knowledge or in action turns out to be the ultimate end but is just a step. The

8 Thomas Aquinas, *Quaestiones disputatae de veritate* 10,12 ad 5: *Summum bonum desideratur dupliciter: uno modo in sui essentia; et sic non omnia desiderant summum bonum; alio modo in sui similitudine; et sic omnia desiderant summum bonum, quia nihil est desiderabile nisi in quantum in eo similitudo summi boni invenitur*, 'the highest good is desired in two ways: one way is for itself and in this way not everything desires the highest good; the other is for its likeness and in this way all things desire the highest good, since nothing is desirable unless some likeness of the highest good is found in it'.

9 Thomas Aquinas, *op. cit.*, 22,2: *Et ideo ... propter hoc quod (Deus) est ultimus finis, appetitur in omni fini, sed hoc est appetere ipsum Deum implicite*, 'since God is the ultimate end he is sought in every end; this is to seek God himself implicitly'.

10 Karl Rahner, *Foundations of Christian Faith*, 1978, London, p. 32

answer to every problem is always the beginning of a new question. Human personality experiences itself therefore as infinite possibility, because every result, sought-after and attained, opens up a further horizon.

Rahner teaches that even in the first steps of questioning activity, there must be a presence of the journey's end, the end of all searching. The human mind can distinguish between the specific items it has knowledge of only on the basis of a pre-apprehension of infinite reality, against which every specific issue is measured and found limited. This fundamental implicit communion with unlimited being in the act of knowing is a basic openness in a person's nature to the mystery of being, which is God. Hence, there is a pre-reflective, pre-apprehension of God inbuilt into our very nature. Rahner calls this 'transcendental revelation'. Consequently, he maintains that every time we reach beyond ourselves – for instance in acts of selfless love, in the experience of beauty, in following what is true and good whatever the cost, in acts of trust and hope – we are experiencing and responding to grace mediated through the specific. God has designed us for communion with him within the Trinity: 'that they all may be one in us', as we read in Chapter 17 of John. Therefore part of our design structure is an inbuilt reach towards the Absolute. In all this we can make theoretical distinctions between the natural and the supernatural, nature and grace. In actual fact since grace abounds, every search is a graced action. For the preacher Rahner has this to say: 'Preaching is the awakening and making explicit of what is already there in the depths of man, not by nature but by grace. Grace enfolds man, the sinner and the unbeliever too, as his very sphere of existence which he can never escape from[11].

JÜRGEN HABERMAS

Coming from a totally different, non-theological background, the German philosopher, Jürgen Habermas, says something that sounds familiar following the two previous writers. He distinguishes between practical reason and technical reason. Technical reason is involved in science, technology, and administration while practical reason relates to human control,

11 Karl Rahner, *Nature and Grace*, 1963, London, Sheed and Ward, p. 32

needs, and interests. He would say that the practical has been collapsed into the technical and there is no real human control over our destiny. As he puts it, '... no attempt ... is made to attain a rational consensus on the part of citizens with the practical control of their destiny. Its place is taken by the attempt to attain technical control over history...'[12]. How can one transcend limited, distorted forms of life and emancipate oneself? The first thing we have to accept is that the present situation is not an absolute. It is only one historical expression of human life. We can discover a much freer situation in which there is full and unrestrained communication; in which one finds truth, freedom, and justice; in which there is fair argumentation, 'which is completely free of compulsion and in which only the force of the better argument may prevail[13]. How do we set about this? We do so by criticizing the assumed consensus in the light of rationally determined consensus. Whence do we dream up the rationally determined consensus? In all communication there is an anticipated and presupposed presence of this consensus. Habermas says: 'No matter how the inter-subjectivity of mutual understanding may be deformed, the design of an ideal speech situation is necessarily implied in the structure of potential speech, since all speech, even of intentional deception, is orientated towards the idea of truth'.[14]

GEORGE STEINER

George Steiner writes about aesthetics. A work of art comes to the observer from without. It changes her life, questions her attitudes, opens to her new possibilities of life, unsettles, darkens, and gives light. It does so because what human consciousness encounters in great music, literature, and art is objective reality at its most primordial. Steiner writes: 'I want to ask whether a hermeneutics and a reflex of valuation – the encounter with meaning in the verbal sign, in the painting, in the musical composition, and the assessment of the quality of such meaning in respect of form – can be made intelligible, can be made answerable

12 Jürgen Habermas, *Theory and Practice*, 1973, Boston, p.255
13 M.Pusey, *Jürgen Habermas*, 1987, Chichester, p.73
14 Jürgen Habermas, 'Towards a Theory of Communicative Competence', *Inquiry*, 13 (1970), p.372

to the existential facts, if they do not imply, if they do not contain, a postulate of transcendence'.[15] He describes this postulate of transcendence as 'verification transcendent'. He cannot prove it but it is the only intuition that will fit the facts. This intuition is built around the theme of creativity itself. A work of art, be it music, literature, painting, or whatever, is not mimetic. The urge that drove Michelangelo to tap a human form from cold stone was not a struggle to represent exactly the model he was working from. He was rather a second creator in tune with the forces that produced the universe in the first place. He was standing before the stone in transcendent presence so that what was produced is unique, questioning, formed, and unsettling. It is like nothing that was there before; it is certainly not an imitation of anything. Because of the presence that possessed him, the statue becomes a focus of creating power. The strength of the work of art to enthral and change us comes precisely from that presence which it brings into our lives. It is an experience of the Kingdom among us, Luke 17:21.

What has all this to do with the silent misery of a hospital bed or the anger of someone who feels betrayed, cast adrift, and lost? Aquinas, Rahner, Habermas, and Steiner represent a broad spectrum of thought on the human condition. Their teachings seem to indicate that all parties in the preaching event have more in common than they might suspect. The journey to transcendence is the path trod by every man and woman. The roadmaps may differ but the grace-enhanced human search for love, fulfilment, and meaning is much the same.

The task of the preacher is not to provide answers. The deeper the alienation, the more poignant the distress, the more evident is the poverty of words. The 'preacher' in difficult times is inevitably asked the question. 'what sense does this make?', 'why me?', 'where is God in all this?' Again and again the safest and most trust-building reply is to say quite honestly 'I really don't know'. In two books of the Old Testament, profound thinkers, Job and Qoheleth, retain their faith while standing by the abyss of darkness. Qoheleth's restless, unorthodox questioning blitzes the anodynes of conventional wisdom and religion. Attempts have been made

15 George Steiner, *Real Presences*, 1989, London, p.134

to rationalise the contradictions in Qoheleth by attributing them to interpolations designed to soften the impact of the original text. More appropriately they are the product of a deep mind which believes that truth is a zone somewhere between contradictions and that understanding is not found in well worked out answers but in the formulation and holding of questions[16]. At the end of Job's anger, bitterness, and protest, he is left not with clarity but only with faith in a God whose schemes are too vast for him to understand.

For Thomas Aquinas the ultimate insight we can have into God is to know that we do not know him[17]. Karl Rahner writes of the 'the vast silent desert of the Godhead',[18] of 'the uncharted terrifying remoteness of the God'.[19] Recently Nicholas Lash wrote: 'the closer we are drawn to God, the more that we begin to gain some understanding of the holy mystery of God, the more what we say and what we do refracts the character of God's Word, the more conscious we become of the depths of our unknowing. God becomes more unknown, not less, the more we understand Him. That is why the tradition speaks of "*docta ignorantia*" of "educated ignorance"'.[20] Some standard words, meant to comfort, may be of no real help: 'God has his purposes', 'it is God's will'. We do not

16 Carol Newsom writes: 'Since one of Qohelet's themes is the inability of human enterprise to seize and hold, to take possession of a thing, it is perhaps no accident that the book eludes the attempts of interpretive activity to fix its meaning determinately. I think that scholars have underestimated the significance of interpretive ambiguity in Ecclesiastes by seeing it as merely a problem to be solved. Perhaps it should be seen instead as another means of communicating the book's message', in J.L. Mays, D. Petersen, K.H. Richards, (edd.) *Old Testament Interpretation Past, Present, and Future* 1995, Edinburgh, T& T Clark, p. 190

17 Thomas Aquinas, *Quaestiones disputatae de potentia Dei* 7,5 ad 14: *et propter hoc illud est ultimum cognitionis humanae de Deo quod sciat se Deum nescire,* 'and so the ultimate in human knowledge of God is that s/he knows him/herself as not knowing God'.

18 Karl Rahner, "Poetry and the Christian", *Theological Investigations IV*, 1966, Baltimore, Helicon Press, and London, Darton, Longman and Todd p.359

19 Karl Rahner, "Priest and Poet", *Theological Investigations IV*, 1966, Baltimore, Helicon Press, and London, Darton, Longman and Todd, p.309

20 Nicholas Lash, *Holiness, Speech and Silence. Reflections on the Question of God*, 2004, Aldershot, Ashgate, p.76

know what his purpose is in this or what his will is. All we know is that he stands with us in suffering and that love has a focal point in the 'preacher' there in the circle of pain.

As every parent knows, it is touch, not words that mollifies a child's distress. In times of darkness, our human instinct is to comfort and to hold in love. In similar circumstances, the preacher's art is to bring friendship and caring support for the journey. On that road to Emmaus the mysterious traveller brought insight into the scriptures, 'he interpreted to them in all the scriptures the things concerning himself', Luke 24:27. He 'went with them', 24:15. It all happened 'on the road', 24:32,35 and their hearts burned as he talked with them, 24:32. Things were said, understanding was shared, lives were changed, but all in the context of journeying with, of friendship, and of hospitality. In that way the distressed, the alienated, and the preacher travel together. They walk the same road even when the earth moves and their worlds collapse.

XI

The Fourth Friend:
Poetry in a Time of Affliction

PAUL MURRAY, OP

THE FOURTH FRIEND:
POETRY IN A TIME OF AFFLICTION

Paul Murray, OP

W hat, if anything, consoles us in a time of affliction? Today we don't need to look very far to see that our own generation is living through such a time, and this is true whether we are living in Europe or in Iraq, in Sudan or in the Middle East, in Egypt or in the United States. As far as the West is concerned, we have only to think back to the horrific bombings in the station at Madrid in 2004, or to recall the shock and horror of 9/11 in 2001. But there have been other horrors, other scenes of humiliation and terror, which we have witnessed on our television screens, the most notable of all, of course, the effect of the 2004 tsunami earthquake. Although these events may have taken place thousands of miles away, they too have seared our imagination. My question, then, is this: in such a time of affliction, of what possible use to us is poetry? Can it be said to help or console us in any way?

After 9/11, there was, as it happens, one remarkable, instinctive response of the people in New York, a response manifest not only in and around Ground Zero, but also in many of the streets of the city. For, on the walls of the city, in the subway, in the side-walks, there began to appear lines from famous poems, and even entire original poems, written up and pinned to photographs of some of the men and women who had died in the catastrophe. One account from *The New York Times*, written some time after the collapse of the towers, included the following observation:

> In the weeks since the terrorist attacks, people have been consoling themselves – and one another – in an almost unprecedented manner. Almost immediately..., improvised memorials often conceived around poems, sprang up all over the city, in store windows, at bus stops, in Washington Square Park, Brooklyn Heights, and elsewhere. And poems flew through cyberspace across the country in e-mails from friend to friend[1].

---

1 Dinitia Smith, 'In Shelly or Auden, in the Sonnet or Free Verse, The Eerily Intimate Power of Poetry to Console', *New York Times*, Monday, 1 October 2001, p.E1.

The poet laureate of the United States, Billy Collins, found that, after September 11, he was inundated with poems from friends. And he remarked: 'It's interesting that people don't turn to the novel or say, "We should all go out to a movie", or "Ballet would help us". It's always poetry. What we want to hear is a human voice speaking directly in our ear'.[2] A human voice, an intimate voice, the voice of a friend. With respect to the title of the present paper, one phrase requires explanation. The question needs to be asked: why the fourth friend?

In the history of religious literature, and indeed in the history of literature itself, there is one figure – one man – who can be said to represent the afflicted human being. And that is, of course, Job in the Old Testament. Job is the innocent and good man punished by misfortune and sickness. In chapter two of The Book of Job we read of how he suffers 'with malignant tumors from the sole of his foot to the top of his head' (2:7). Further, we read that 'the news of all the disasters that had fallen on Job came to the ears of three of his friends', and they decided to go to him at once to 'offer him sympathy and consolation' (2:11). But Job finds no comfort whatever in their long, rational, and somewhat boring speeches. He exclaims at one point:

> What sorry comforters you are!
> Is there never an end of airy words?
> What a plague your need is to have the last word! (16:2-3)

Job's three lugubrious friends, far from bringing him 'sympathy and consolation', seem to have brought him instead more misery and distress. But then, all of a sudden, a fourth friend, a figure often strangely overlooked by readers and exegetes, arrives on the scene. Victor White, the Oxford Dominican, calls him 'something of an intuitive, a poet'.[3] Of this fourth arrival, he writes: 'Then comes Elihu, the fourth friend...[who] stresses the vastness and incomprehensibility of God and the limitations of the conscious human standpoint'.[4] This fourth friend is at pains, we are told by

---

2 ibid.

3 Victor White, OP, 'Jung on Job', Blackfriars, Vol.XXXVI, n° 420 (March 1955) p.53.

4 ibid.

White, to silence 'the rationalistic and moralistic chatter' of the three other so-called friends, Job's would-be comforters. He, Elihu, emphasises that 'the ways of God are beyond wordy explanations'.[5] God, he insists – and here he sounds very much like a poet – communicates not by rational explanations but 'by dreams, and visions that come in the night, when slumber comes on mankind, and men are all asleep in bed' (33:15-16).

Elihu presents himself then, in Victor White's understanding, as a kind of poet. But what Elihu goes on to say, though a matter of no small interest and importance, is not – given the limitations of this short paper – my own immediate or principal concern. I introduce the figure of Elihu here for one reason only, and that is to introduce the theme and title of this paper. For, in the presence of Job, the archetypal figure of affliction, Elihu stands as a figure or symbol of all those poets or writers who dare to speak in the presence of great affliction. Elihu himself exclaims at one point:

> Now I will have my say,
>   my turn has come to say what I know.
> For I am filled with words,
>   choked by the rush of them within me …
> Nothing will bring relief but speech (32:17-18).

But should the poet, in a time of affliction, presume to speak at all? Are words, any words, ever adequate at such a time? Do they not, in some sense, inevitably betray the very reality they are attempting to describe? And how, confronted by the enormous affliction of an individual or of a people, can the words of a poet be said to bring consolation?

In her celebrated poem entitled 'Requiem', the Russian poet, Anna Akmatova, recalls the many women – mothers and widows like herself – whose sons and husbands were imprisoned, tortured and murdered during the years of terror in Communist Russia. The poem is introduced by a short prose passage. It reads:

> During the terrible years of the Yezhov terror I spent seventeen months in the prison queues in Leningrad. One day someone 'identified' me. Then a woman with lips blue

---

5 *ibid.* See Job 33:13.

with cold who was standing behind me, and of course had never heard of my name, came out of the numbness which affected us all and whispered in my ear – (we all spoke in whispers there): 'Could you describe this?' I said 'I can!' Then something resembling a smile slipped over what had once been her face[6].

The poem itself, the entire poem, is remarkable, and not least for the fact that it seems to breathe throughout a spirit of forgiveness. (Akmatova was a devout Orthodox Christian.) But, in this extract, Akmatova declares that she cannot forget, will not forget, the dreadful suffering endured by so many innocent men and women. Her task, as she understands it, is to remember and to pray. She writes:

This woman is sick,
this woman is alone,
husband in the grave, son in prison,
pray for me[7].

And again:

I pray not for myself alone,
but for everyone who stood with me
in the cruel cold, in the July heat,
under the blinded, red wall[8].

Akmatova is referring here to the long queues of women who waited for hours and hours in the cold outside the prison walls in Leningrad, hoping against hope they might be allowed to visit, even once, their sons, husbands, brothers. Here, though brought face to face in memory with the inhuman, the unspeakable, Akmatova dares to speak. She is compelled to speak. Remembering the extreme cold, and the long wait, and the ravaged faces of the women standing, hour after hour, outside the prison wall, she writes:

---

6 Anna Akmatova, 'Instead of a Forward' Requiem: Poems 1935-1940, in Anna Akmatova: *Selected Poems*, trans. R. McKane (Newcastle upon Tyne 1989) p.281.

7 Akmatova, Requiem: Poems 1935-1940, p.283.

8 *ibid.*, p.287.

The hour of remembrance has drawn close again.
I see you, hear you, feel you:

the one they could hardly get to the window,
the one who no longer walks on this earth,

the one who shook her beautiful head,
and said: 'Coming here is like coming home.'

I would like to name them all but they took away
the list and there's no way of finding them.

For them I have woven a wide shroud
from the humble words I heard among them.

I remember them always, everywhere,
I will never forget them, whatever comes.

And if they gag my tormented mouth
with which one hundred million people cry,

then let them also remember me
on the eve of my remembrance day.

If they ever think of building
a memorial to me in this country,

I consent to be so honoured,
only with this condition: not to build it

near the sea where I was born:
my last tie with the sea is broken,

nor in the Tsar's Garden by the hallowed stump
where an inconsolable shadow seeks me,

but here, where I stood three hundred hours
and they never unbolted the door for me.

since even in blessed death I am terrified
that I will forget the thundering of Black Marias,

forget how the hateful door slammed,
how an old woman howled like a wounded beast.

Let the melting snow stream
like tears from my bronze eyelids,

let the prison dove call in the distance
and the boats go quietly on the Neva[9].

9 *ibid.*, pp.287-88.

One of the women standing in the queue outside the prison yard had asked Anna Akmatova: 'Could you describe this?' And Akmatova replied 'Yes'. Later, when actually describing the experience in her poem, 'Requiem', Akmatova achieved two things: first of all, she remembered the details of all that happened, and, second, and perhaps most important of all, in the effort to find words to speak the unspeakable, she named the experience, named the unnamable. And that, in itself, was of course an enormous achievement. Joseph Brodsky, speaking of Akmatova, writes: 'At certain periods of history it is only poetry that is capable of dealing with reality by condensing it into something graspable, something that otherwise couldn't be retained by the mind'.[10]

On the subject of naming I am reminded here of a humble text – humble from the strictly literary point of view – which was given to me by a woman who had been sexually abused when she was a young child. Needless to say, she had no name to give to the experience that was happening to her. She was four years old. But, years later, when she began slowly to be healed by God's grace, the child within her whose pain she had repressed for so long, began at last to reveal what had happened, and began to remember, and found courage to speak the unspeakable. This young woman was not, I hasten to add here, a writer or poet of any note or pretension, but she is a remarkable person. It was my privilege to have known her, as a spiritual friend, during the years in which, step by step, she came to terms with her wounded history. Now, several years later, she is, I am glad to report, as radiant and joyful a person as ever one could hope to meet. The text of hers I want to quote now was written during that demanding and extraordinarily vulnerable but also wonderful time when healing really began to take place. It is entitled 'The Stone with No Name'.

THE STONE WITH NO NAME

I look at the child
and the child looks at me.
Her eyes are looking into the void,
into the void of her heart.

10 Joseph Brodsky, 'Introduction', in Anna Akmatova: *Poems*, trans. L. Coffin (New York 1981) p.xxx.

On her heart
is a heavy stone … a black stone
which doesn't allow her to breathe,
a stone with no name
which was placed there
on a sunlit day
when, all of a sudden, night
fell at midday.

She has a story to tell,
a sad story, a true story and I
believe her.
When she speaks, the stone
becomes lighter.
The stone has a name
now. She has revealed
the name to me.

One day the stone
will become a golden stone,
the precious stone of her
sepulcher.
The stone will be lifted away
by God's grace.

And she will rise
from her sepulcher on that sunlit
day, and I will
sit on the stone, and she
will sit on my lap
and I will embrace her
and she will embrace me.

And we will become one
on that day…
we will be able to breathe.

This young woman, though not a poet in any ordinary sense of
the word, found herself instinctively turning to verse or poetry as
a form of expression when trying, with all her strength and courage,
to live through the most challenging and demanding time of her

life. It is, I think, for good reason that Henry Vaughan, the English seventeenth century poet, could declare in one of his verses: 'Afflictions turn our blood to ink'.[11] The sustained, unusual affliction endured by the great Jesuit poet, Gerard Manley Hopkins, during the last years of his life, when he was living and working in Dublin, found expression in what is, in my judgment, the most remarkable poetry of affliction ever composed in the English language. Not surprisingly, the poems themselves are known as 'the despair sonnets'. Hopkins, in his anguish, finds that the God whom, as a younger man, he had loved and worshipped, and who seemed so immanent to his life and work, has now simply disappeared. All his prayers and laments no longer attain to the object of his love. Here is a stanza from one of the sonnets. It opens with the light of a new day dawning. But Hopkins wakes up to find himself in an almost total mental and spiritual darkness:

> I wake and feel the fell of dark, not day.
> What hours, O what black hours we have spent
> This night! what sights you, heart, saw; ways you went!
> And more must, in yet longer light's delay.
>   With witness I speak this. But where I say
> Hours I mean years, mean life. And my lament
> Is cries countless, cries like dead letters sent
> To dearest him that lives alas! Away[12]

Part of what Gerard Manley Hopkins was undergoing in those last terrible years in Dublin was, I have no doubt, the experience referred to sometimes as the dark night of the soul. The absence of God, therefore, or what seemed like absence, was in reality an experience of overwhelming grace: God utterly present in the soul and yet utterly hidden. This experience has been described, perhaps best of all, in the poetry and prose of St John of the Cross. John's first great poems were written at a time of utter desolation in his life. Attempting, with St Teresa of Avila, to start a reform of the

---

11 Henry Vaughan, 'On Sir Thomas Bodley's Library; the Author Being Then in Oxford', *The Complete Poems*, ed. A. Rudrum (Harmondsworth 1976) p.336.

12 Gerard Manley Hopkins, *A Selection of His Poems and Prose*, ed. W.H. Gardner (Harmondsworth 1963) p.62.

Carmelite Order, he was imprisoned by some of the unreformed brothers, beaten, tortured, and almost starved to death. But it was there, in that situation of complete affliction, that John found his voice as a poet. And the poems he began to write are considered among the greatest mystical verse ever composed. One of the poems he wrote opens with a cry of spiritual desolation:

> My Love, where are you hidden?
> Why have you left me sorrowing alone?
> I followed you unbidden,
> but like a stag you'd flown:
> wounded, I called, but you, my Love, were gone[13].

The one who is speaking is the Bride, the soul, and her lament, her appeal, continues:

> This heart you have enraptured –
> why leave it sorely wounded? Why not heal?
> Taken by force and captured,
> Beloved, I appeal –
> why not bear off the prey you swooped to steal?
>
> Quench all my grief! Draw near!
> Your touch alone brings comfort in my plight.
> Light of my eyes, appear!
> You are indeed their light,
> and for your sake alone I guard my sight.
>
> Show me your face, my Lover,
> even though beauty seen unveiled should kill,
> let it be so! Discover
> your presence, if you will,
> at once the cause and cure of all my ill[14].

At this point in the poem, or just after it, there occurs a moment of illumination. John is made suddenly aware that the Beloved is present. And he – or the Bride – stunned by the grace of the moment, begins to sing with quiet ecstasy: the beauty of the Beloved wonderfully evoked by an identification of his presence with the beauty of nature.

13 St John of the Cross, 'The Spiritual Canticle', trans. M. Flower (Adelaide 1983) p.11.
   14 *ibid.*, p.12.

> My beloved, the mountains,
> the solitary wooded valleys, the strange
> islands, the resounding rivers,
> the whisper of the amorous breezes,
> the tranquil night.
> At the time
> of the rising of the dawn, the silent music,
> the sounding solitude,
> the supper that refreshes and deepens love[15].

Even in translation these lines are memorable. It is no wonder that St John believed that some of his poems were, on occasion, directly inspired by God. And John never made this claim concerning his prose. That the poems survived at all to see the light of day is itself a kind of miracle. When John finally escaped from prison – and he did so by tying together the blankets from his bed, and making a great leap – he brought nothing with him but his poems. It was very early in the morning, and John made his way to a small convent of enclosed contemplatives – a group of Carmelite nuns who had remained faithful to Teresa's reform. They welcomed him at once, and brought him straight into the cloister to hide him, although of course this was completely against Canon Law. (The splendid excuse they evoked was that one of the sick sisters, who was bed-ridden, needed to go to confession!) John was so exhausted he could hardly stand, and could barely speak. He was the image of death. The nuns fed him pears stewed in cinnamon, the only food he could digest. Then, suddenly, a group of the unreformed friars arrived with some constables, *alguaciles*, searching for him. But, of course, they did not dare violate the cloister. As soon as they had gone, the sisters led John into the chapel. But in the chapel something unusual happened. Although John could speak only in a whisper, and could barely stand, he recited there and then for the nuns some of the poems he had composed in prison, a clear indication of how much he valued them.

---

15 This is a (slightly) revised version of the lines as they appear in the translation by E. Allison Peers, *The Complete Works of Saint John of the Cross*, Vol.1 (Wheathampstead 1974) p.181.

Some time later it was decided that John should be sent to a remote priory in Spain where he could escape from the clutches of his enemies. On the way there, he made an extended visit to another convent of the sisters loyal to Teresa, the convent of Beas de Segura. One day, during his visit, when John was sitting with the contemplative nuns in the parlour – it was the time of recreation – the superior asked one of the younger sisters to sing a few verses of a song. She began:

> The one who knows nothing of pains
> in this valley of sorrows
> knows nothing of good things
> nor has tasted of love
> since pains are the garments of lovers[16].

Hearing this song, John was at once overcome with emotion. He signalled for the sister to cease, and stood, gripping with both hands the bars of the grill. Tears, we are told, poured down his cheeks. For an hour, John remained there, standing against the grill, unable to speak or to move. Later, recovering himself, he told the sisters that although, when he was in prison, God had made clear to him the great value of suffering, he had been able to offer only a small part of what he had endured to God.

There is, in the Hebrew Bible, one particular psalm with which a prisoner in John's situation, or indeed any innocent prisoner, would at once identify. It is Psalm 137. The psalm begins with the famous lament of the Jewish prisoners in Babylon:

> By the waters of Babylon
> we sat down and wept, remembering Zion.
> On the poplars that grew there
> we hung up our harps…
> For how could we sing
> the song of the Lord on alien soil? (137:1-2,4)

During the months when John found himself on the 'alien soil' of his own prison, he wrote a version of this psalm in Spanish, a sort of ballad. Here are the first two verses of John's version, translated of course into English:

16 This is a (slightly) revised version of the translation which appears in *St John of the Cross: His Life and Poetry* by Gerald Brennan (Cambridge 1973) p.41.

Beside the flowing river
That in Babylon I found
I sat and there with weeping
Watered foreign ground.

Recalling thee, O Zion,
Beloved by me so well;
The sweetness of thy memory
Increased the tears that fell[17].

Like many people in extreme situations, John of the Cross found himself turning instinctively to poems or songs or stories that he remembered from the past. And more recently, the famous modern prisoner, the Dutch woman Etty Hillesum, in the last entry she wrote in her diary before being taken finally to the concentration camp, spoke of the surprising encouragement she received, in that dark time, from reading the poems of the German poet, Rainer Maria Rilke. 'I always return to Rilke',[18] she wrote. Far too easily we 'shrug off', she declared, 'the spiritual heritage' of poets and artists such as Rilke, saying to ourselves, 'What use is that sort of thing to us now?' But, in fact, she asserted, 'in turbulent and debilitating times', we can and should turn to the poets for 'support and a ready response to [our] bewildered questions'.[19] The nature of that 'response' to our questions is, of course, something mysterious. What the poets offer us is clearly not a book of answers, nor a vadecum of fixed, rational explanations.

A man I knew in Dublin, a few years ago, suffered enormous distress after the death from meningitis of his beautiful young daughter, Eva, his only child. I had occasion to meet him over a number of weeks and, at one point, lent him a book of poems by a Polish sixteenth century author who had himself been devastated by the death of his own youngest child. The book was called Laments, and the author's name, Jan Kochanowski. I cannot say for sure that reading these poems consoled my friend, but it gave

17 St John of the Cross, 'Ballad on the Psalm "By the Waters of Babylon"', trans., L. Nicholson, in Gerald Brennan, St John of the Cross: His Life and Poetry (Cambridge 1973) p.183.
18 Etty Hillesum, Etty: A Diary 1941-43, trans., A.J. Pomerans (London 1983) p.196.
19 ibid.

him a support of a kind he found almost nowhere else. Kochanowski is regarded as, by far, the greatest Slavic poet up to the beginning of the nineteenth century, and *Laments*, is his most achieved work. Here is one of the poems, in a fine translation by the Irish poet, Seamus Heaney:

LAMENT 8

The void that fills my house is so immense
Now that my girl is gone. It baffles sense:
We all are here, yet no one is, I feel;
The flight of one small soul has tipped the scale.
You talked for all of us, you sang for all,
You played in every nook and cubbyhole.
You never would have made your mother brood
Nor father think too much for his own good;
The house was carefree. Everybody laughed.
You held us in your arms: our hearts would lift.
Now emptiness reigns here; the house is still;
Nobody ever laughs nor ever will.
All your old haunts have turned to haunts of pain,
And every heart is hankering in vain[20].

Speaking on one occasion to a group of writers, John XXIII remarked: 'what characterizes you above all else in the eyes of the general public is your means of expression, your language. The language of the poet, the man of letters, and the musician is particularly apt for laying bare the secret places of the soul, for interpreting its suffering and consoling its suffering'.[21] It is worth noting that Pope John speaks here not only of the language of the poet, and of its power to console, but also of the language of the musician. So far, here, I have given attention only to the potential gift of poetry in a time of affliction. But that is not to deny for a moment the mysterious blessing that music, when it is played or sung, can on occasion bring to the troubled mind or to the wounded heart.

20 Jan Kochanowski, *Laments*, trans. S. Heaney and S. Baraczak (London 1995) p.17.
21 Pope John XXIII, 'Extract from an Address to the International Confederation of Societies of Authors and Composers', in *Catholics on Literature*, ed., J.C. Whitehouse (Dublin 1997) p.177. The Address was published originally in *Acta Apostolicae Sedis* 3 (1962) pp.518-20.

There is one instance which comes to mind here of the way music can interpret our suffering, and even bring us consolation. A friend of Beethoven's, Dorothea von Ertmann, lost first one of her children, then another, and then another, until all her small children were dead. Not long afterwards Beethoven invited Dorothea to come to his house, and what happened then she described later to the composer, Felix Mendelssohn. Fortunately, Mendelssohn remembered what she said, and wrote about the incident in a letter which he sent to the composer, Hayden, in the summer of 1831. Here is what he wrote:

She [Dorothea] told me that when she lost her last child, Beethoven was at first unable to come to her house any more. Finally, he invited her to come to him, and when she came he sat at the piano and merely said: 'We will now converse in music', and played for over an hour and, as she expressed it, 'He said everything to me, and also finally gave me consolation'.[22]

No small part of that 'consolation' is, I would say, the fact that the experience of loss, for the space of an hour, was acknowledged and somehow evoked by the music, by that unique swelling of sound which is itself a kind of inarticulate, unfathomable speech. The affliction was named; it was given a voice.

But with respect, in general, to the communication of poetry or music at this level, there is obviously something more than a mere naming involved. For, confronted with an individual person suffering enormous grief, for example, a listener such as a gifted psychologist, or even a journalist, can in some measure name the experience. But a work of art, when it takes the form of music or of painting or of poetry, does something else as well, something different, something more. And that 'something more' is what explains, in great measure, the consolation which it brings.

But how to describe this phenomenon? The best word, the simplest word, the word which points to the distinctive nature of art, and to the wondrous power it has over us, is of course the word 'beauty'. I cited a few moments ago the lament by Jan Kochanowski for his young daughter, Orszula, a short poem, but

22 See Letter of Mendelssohn to Hayden, 14 July 1831, in *Beethoven* by H.C. Robbins Landon (London 1970) p.196.

one which was able to describe with great vividness the experience of grief and loss. Reading over this poem it soon becomes apparent that the work not only speaks about the experience of grief and loss, it not only names the experience for the reader, it also somehow sings. Encountering a work of art of this kind, we are made aware of two things: on the one hand, the anguish of the man who has suffered, and is still suffering, and on the other hand, the sense of an almost serene detachment in the work itself. Yes, the experience described is unspeakably sad, but the form of the poem, its incantation, its music – while in no way denying the sadness, the heart-break – is somehow able, for the space of the poem, to lift the heart with its beauty, and bring a kind of peace.

But there is a mystery here. For, however often we hear that redemptive music in a work of art, in Mozart's 'Requiem' for example, or in the 'Requiem' by Anna Akmatova, or in the tiny 'Lament' by Jan Kochanowski, we seem always unable to understand how it has been achieved. Somehow the great artist can contemplate the lineaments of sorrow in a world of chaos and suffering, and yet still create out of this material a thing of matchless beauty. Even in the poetry of the most profound sorrow and lament, if the work is of the highest order, there is always somewhere – if you look for it – a lift in the words, an element of praise, a singing line. This truth is one that found expression once in a short poem by Rainer Maria Rilke. It occurs to me now that the poem in question may well have been one of the verses by Rilke that helped sustain Etty Hillesum at the end.

> Tell us, poet, what is your task?
>   I praise.
> But the murderous things, the monstrous things,
> how do you endure them, how can you bear them?
>   I praise.
> But the mysteries which are anonymous and nameless,
> how, poet, can you still invoke them?
>   I praise.
> By what right can you presume, in all your disguises,
> and in every kind of mask, to remain true?
>   I praise.

And how is it that both stillness and turbulence
know you like star and storm?
                              Because I praise[23].

I began this paper concerning poetry in a time of affliction by speaking about Job. And I suggested that Elihu, the fourth friend, might be considered a sort of poet, and could therefore be made to stand as a figure or symbol of all the poets and artists who have dared to speak in the presence of affliction. But, of course, the real poet, and the one who speaks about affliction like almost no one else in the history of religious literature, is the anonymous Hebrew author who composed the Book of Job itself. Robert Altar, in his introduction to The Literary Guide to the Bible, suggests that 'the very pinnacle of ancient Hebrew poetry was reached in Job'.[24] That is, I think, a wise judgment, and it is one well worth remembering when we consider that the Author behind the author, the Poet behind the poet of the Book of Job, is none other than God himself.

In a time of affliction, we instinctively look to the Word of God for answers, for explanations. But often the kind of answers we want, the explanations we expect, are not forthcoming. There are, of course, great and saving statements given to us, and messages of enormous import. But, for some reason, instead of communicating his Word to us with the clear and distinct ideas of a scholastic treatise, God prefers very often, it would appear, to speak through short stories, parables and poems. No wonder the South American writer, Jorge Luis Borges, could exclaim, 'Jesus, the man of Nazareth never uses arguments. He uses metaphor.' Now Borges may be exaggerating here, for there is an unmistakable body of teaching in all the four Gospels. Nevertheless, it has to be said, that in the Gospels, as in many other books of the Bible (in the

---

23 Translation of the Rilke poem, 'O sag, Dicher, was du tust?', by Jurg Schmid and Paul Murray.

24 *The Literary Guide to the Bible*, eds. R. Altar and F. Kermode (Cambridge, Massachusetts 1987) p.15. The greatest passages of poetry in the Book of Job are not those delivered by Yahweh or those addressed to Job by the young, 'intuitive' Elihu. They are the remarkable speeches voiced for Job himself. Although Elihu, the fourth friend, may perhaps be considered 'a kind of poet', he is not of the same order as Job. His speeches contain, it has to be admitted, almost as many 'airy words' as those of the first three comforters.

Psalms for example, and in the Book of Job itself) God is doing far more than merely handing down to us a moral and doctrinal message. And this is especially true with regard to the question of affliction. For, in this matter, God speaks to us more like a poet than a scientific theologian. And so, just as with a number of the poems we have been considering here, so also in these books of the Bible, in these saving parables and poems and stories, we find that our affliction is named. And that, in itself, marks the beginning of our souls' healing, and the beginning also, I would say, of our inner conversion.

In the Book of Job, God does not give us answers to the mystery of affliction any more than Beethoven gave answers to his grieving friend, Dorothea von Ertmann. But by naming, through poems and stories, the black stone of affliction – the stone which had no name, perhaps, but which weighed heavily on our hearts – the weight of the stone is somehow lifted. We are touched by God's grace, and healing begins. God is our teacher – that goes without saying. He is Truth itself, and he is Goodness. But he is also Beauty, 'beauty's self and beauty's giver',[25] as Hopkins puts it. And that means that, in the book of his living Word, in the Bible, as well as teaching us truth and goodness, he is also trying to heal and awaken us in much the same way as a work of art or a piece of music will sometimes pierce us with its beauty. On one occasion, Simone Weil remarked: 'The soul's natural inclination to love beauty is the trap God most frequently uses in order to win it and open it to the breath from high'.[26]

There comes to mind here a phrase from the writings of Fyodor Dostoyevsky, a phrase or statement which has been acknowledged by many people, over the years, as a wondrous, necessary phrase. Dostoyevsky, we know, at certain times in his life, found himself, as a man and an author, forced to confront scenes of unspeakable sadness and horror, scenes comparable to those we ourselves witness today. And yet, in his writings, he declared – and in the

25 Hopkins, 'The Leaden Echo and the Golden Echo', p.54.

26 Simone Weil, *Waiting on God*, trans. E. Craufurd (Glasgow 1950) p.118. It is no accident that Augustine uses the word 'beauty' rather than any other word in his famous cry: 'Late, late, have I loved you, O Beauty ever ancient and ever new!' *Confessions*, X, 27.

teeth, it seemed, of all the evidence – 'Beauty will save the world'.[27]
Now that is an extraordinary claim. God, it is true, often comes to
us, in his Word, like a teacher, and comes to us with a word of
challenge. But when we find ourselves in affliction, is it not the
case that he comes to us in a more humble way, the way Ludwig
van Beethoven came to his grieving friend, Dorothea? Is it not the
case that, in and through his Word, he sits down with us, as it were,
and through his own poems and parables and stories, speaks to
our heart? Let us note, then, once again, by way of conclusion to
this paper, the short, remarkable extract from Mendelssohn's letter
concerning Beethoven:

> Finally, he invited her to come to him, and when she came he
> sat at the piano and merely said: "We will now converse in
> music", and played for over an hour and, as she expressed it,
> "He said everything to me, and also finally gave me
> consolation".[28]

---

27 Dostoyevsky, *The Idiot*, Part III, chap.5.

28 See Letter of Mendelssohn to Hayden, 14 July 1831, in *Beethoven* by H.C.
Robbins Landon (London 1970) p.196.

XII

Grace and Justice:
Preaching and Morality

ARCHIE CONLETH BYRNE, OP

GRACE AND JUSTICE:
PREACHING AND MORALITY

Archie Conleth Byrne, OP

While a student in Tallaght in the 1950s, I remember being told that, as Dominican preachers, we were being prepared for 'doctrinal preaching'. We could have taken this to mean, by implication, that we would leave the more moralistic style of preaching to 'lesser' Orders, like the Redemptorists, or indeed to the secular clergy.

I am sure now that our teachers meant no such thing. Yet, there was some such distinction going back to the infancy of our Order. While the early Franciscans were allowed to give pious moral exhortations, for his new 'Order of Preachers' Dominic aspired to the kind of magisterial preaching then reserved to bishops and their delegates. It was not long before the Franciscans caught up, however, and the early Dominican preachers no doubt also did their fair share of moralising.

In fact the description 'doctrinal' in no way excludes the preaching of morals, as Aquinas' doctrinal synthesis in the *Summa theologiae* makes abundantly clear. The whole centre of this is devoted to what he calls *materia moralis (Summa theologiae II.II* prologue)*, much bigger in volume than either the section devoted to God and Creation, or that which deals with Christ and the Sacraments. All this *materia moralis* is dealt with by Thomas under the rubric of the rational creature's return to God (*de motu rationalis creaturae in Deum*), having already dealt with God and Creation in the *prima pars* and before going on to deal with Christ as our way of reaching God (*via nobis tendendi in Deum*) in the *tertia pars*. All of this is included under the umbrella of *sacra doctrina*, aiming to impart a knowledge of God, not just in himself, but as the origin and goal of all, particularly of rational creatures, such as we are. There is no conflict between 'doctrinal' and 'moral' here, then, only an invitation to do our moralising under the tutelage of sacred doctrine, inspired by the vision of God, from whom all things come and to whom all return.

VIRTUES: THE ART OF GOOD LIVING

Within this vision Thomas chooses to organise his *materia moralis* according to the order of the virtues, theological and moral, rather than the order of the Ten Commandments, though these are included. He cites Augustine's description of virtue as 'the art of living in the way that is right and proper for human beings'.[1] An art is a skill we either have or develop for doing certain things well, like singing or painting or playing a musical instrument. Thomas sees virtue, the art of right living, as a settled attitude of soul that makes it second nature for a person to do the right thing in whatever area of human life that person is operating. So he describes virtues as 'good habits that incline the person who has them to perform good actions freely'.[2] This last word 'freely', *cum electione*, shows that Thomas is using the word 'habit' in a somewhat different way from the way we speak of habits in English. For us a habit suggests something mechanical, causing us to do something automatically rather than freely and deliberately. So we say someone has a habit of doing something that they do without thinking, like cracking their knuckles, or stroking their beard. Far from limiting our freedom in this way, the kind of habit Thomas calls a virtue allows us to do whatever it inclines us to do with even greater freedom and ease. It makes it something we really want to do with all the ease, fluency and flexibility with which great artists produce great music, or paintings or even great games of football or golf.

This is in line with the other classical definition of virtue adopted by Thomas and his contemporaries: 'a good quality in a person, coming from God, which inclines that person to live well and avoid evil'.[3] This description has the advantage of covering both the properly Christian virtues of faith, hope and charity, as well as other human virtues, like justice and temperance, that we share with all

---

1 Augustine, *De civitate Dei* IV.21; XXII.24, cited by Aquinas at *Summa theologiae* I.II 58, 2. For Aquinas on virtue and virtues see E.M. Atkins and Thomas Williams, edd, *Aquinas: Disputed Questions on the Virtues* Cambridge University Press 2005. For a translation of some of what Aquinas writes about prudence, justice, fortitude and temperance in *Summa theologiae* II.II see Richard J.Regan, *Aquinas: the Cardinal Virtues*, Hackett Publishing Co, Indianapolis, 2005.
2 Thomas Aquinas, *Summa theologiae* I.II 58 4 ad 1. See also I.II 100 9
3 Augustine, *De libero arbitrio* II.19, cited by Aquinas at *ST* I.II 55 4

people of good will. In principle, these latter virtues can be developed by any well-motivated human person, even if that person is not a Christian. They are developed and grow with practice, by acting consistently in a particular way, like being consistently fair and just, or patient, or moderate in all circumstances, over a relatively long period of time. Thus, acquiring these virtues is somewhat like developing a practical skill or art, like learning a trade – such as carpentry – or learning to play the 'cello. In this process practice makes perfect, until eventually it becomes like second nature for the practitioner to do a certain thing properly and well.

Good moral qualities developed in this way are described as 'acquired moral virtues'. This contrasts with the distinctively Christian 'theological virtues', which are described as 'infused'. This means simply that we have to be given these, or they have to be put into us by God, as free gifts of his grace to us. We cannot acquire or develop them in ourselves by our own unaided efforts. Still, once we have them by the grace of God, we have to cooperate with, or use them with personal acts of faith and hope and charity. Done consistently, such acts have the effect of allowing these God-given virtues to become more and more deeply rooted in our souls, until it comes to be like second nature to us to live our Christian faith and hope and charity in practice.

GRACE AND NATURE: THEOLOGICAL AND CARDINAL VIRTUES

While we do this, God's gifts to us of faith, hope and charity will be influencing our other, moral, virtues from within. They will infuse them with their own distinctive Christian spirit and open them up to the gifts and fruits of the Holy Spirit. This will then give even these natural moral virtues a properly Christian character in tune with the virtues of faith, hope and charity, which come to us in the first place as gifts of God's grace. As a result, when we are being fair in our dealings with other people, for example, we are not just prompted by human justice, but also by Christian charity. The people whose rights we respect in justice, we treat also as our brothers and sisters in Christ, loved by us with the same love with which we love God our Father and Jesus His Son and our Brother. When we hold our temper with someone who is causing us great annoyance, we are also going further than just exercising ordinary human restraint. Our faith in Jesus' triumph over evil and death makes us able to imitate his superhuman patience. Again, when we show courage in the face of sickness and death, our hope in the risen Jesus makes this something more than just putting up a humanly brave front in the face of adversity. Our human courage is buoyed up by the Holy Spirit's gift of fortitude (or courage) and is inspired by the Beatitude announced by Jesus 'blessed are those who mourn, for they shall be comforted' (Mt 5:4).

In that way all the different virtues working together in our Christian lives can cause each of us to realise in our own way the claim made by St Paul, 'it is no longer I who live, but Christ who lives in me' (Gal 2:20).

While the properly Christian theological virtues of faith, hope and charity help us more directly, though not exclusively, in our relations with God, the so-called 'moral' virtues have to do more directly, though again not exclusively with how we behave towards ourselves and other human persons. The principal moral virtues are called the cardinal virtues of prudence, justice, fortitude (courage) and temperance. The title 'cardinal' has no connection with the Cardinals of the Roman Church as if these eminent personages were specially noted for the practise of these virtues. The title is derived from the Latin word for a hinge, *cardo*, because these are the four key moral virtues around which all the other moral virtues turn or revolve. Each of them has a family of lesser but no less important virtues grouped around it. These tend to be specialisations of the wider influence for good of one of the four cardinal virtues. Each of them targets a particular sphere of human activity within that covered by the presiding cardinal virtue, like justice or temperance. So, for example, under the umbrella of the cardinal virtue of temperance, which regulates the whole area of pleasure and enjoyment in our human lives, we find a little-known virtue called *eutrapelia*, which moderates our enjoyment of sports and games, to give their enjoyment its due place in our busy lives.

While each of the virtues can be studied and talked about by itself, we should remember that all our Christian and moral virtues are linked and interact with one another in various ways, to bring about a certain organised unity in our lives. Thus the cardinal virtue of prudence presides over all our moral virtues, to help us to discern and decide how we can best practise these other virtues in different circumstances. Love for God and neighbour makes us want to do what is best for them in every situation. But love alone will not tell us what that is precisely. Well-meaning people can wreak havoc and do terrible damage – unless they are guided by prudence.

GOOD INCLINATIONS

The most basic and general principle for our moral lives is 'do good, and avoid evil'. This is also one of our basic moral inclinations as human beings, to look for whatever is good for us and others as human beings, and to try to avoid whatever is bad and harmful to us. This does not stop us from sometimes choosing things that are evil or bad for us. Otherwise there would be no sin in our lives. Sinning means deliberately choosing what we know is wrong or evil. Still, whenever we choose something bad or evil in that way, it is not because it is evil or bad that we choose it. We choose it for the good we see, or think we see, in it, whether for ourselves or for others. This means we do not choose evil because it is evil or bad, but because it appears good to us at the time. So, for example, we can choose to tell lies, not because lying is wrong and bad, but because it gets us out of trouble, or brings us some other advantage. Because this appears good to us at the time, we are prepared to accept the wrong we know goes with it for the sake of the good we expect to gain from it. That is how we can sin, or commit some deliberate wrongdoing. To avoid this we need to be able to discern and distinguish what is really good, for us and other persons, from what only appears to be good, though it is in fact wrong or evil. Prudence gives us the discernment to see clearly the genuine good we have to do in every instance and the determination to get it done in practice.

If it is to be really effective in getting us to do the right thing consistently, however, prudence needs to be backed up by good inclinations in our will and affective powers. These will incline us to choose consistently what is truly good, like chaste love, or fairness in our dealings with others, rather than what is in fact evil, though it presents itself to us as good at the time, like lustful pleasure, or dishonest gains from sharp practice. These good inclinations are what the other moral virtues will give us. Justice, for example, will incline our wills to give other people what is rightfully theirs, rather than cheat and deprive them of their rights for our own advantage. Temperance will keep our bodily desires for pleasure and satisfaction within the proper bounds and prevent them from going to harmful excess, by causing us for example to eat or drink too much. Fortitude will restrain our fears and similar emotions, so that they don't impel us to sacrifice what is truly good for us in order to secure some apparent good like false security. These three, along with prudence, make up the four cardinal virtues: prudence, justice, fortitude and temperance.

JUSTICE: RESPECT FOR OTHERS' RIGHTS

Justice is the special virtue that regulates our relations with one another in society. Because our actions in relation to each other make their own special demands, they also need their own special virtue to ensure they are right and good. That virtue is what we call justice. St Thomas describes justice as 'a consistent willingness always to grant everyone what is his or her due', or as a 'habit or disposition by which someone is always consistently committed to give each and everyone his or her rights'.[4] But what do we mean by rights? What is due to that other person? St Thomas introduces his discussion of justice, *iustitia*, with a short discussion of *ius*, the Latin word for a right or for what is 'due' to another[5]. Rights, he says, depend on a certain equality between the parties concerned. The business of justice is to preserve and restore this equality between and among human persons, as members of human society. The jus- in justice is the same as the jus- in the word 'adjust'. This word means to straighten things out, or to even things up, or arrange them in such a way that the proper equilibrium or balance is maintained or restored between them. That is what justice does for the members of human society in their relations with each other. The opposite, a state of imbalance or gross inequality among the members of any society, makes that an unjust society.

The rights which justice inclines us to respect may be based on our natural equality as human beings, all made in the image and

4 Thomas Aquinas, *Summa theologiae* II.II 58 1
5 *op. cit.*, II.II 57

likeness of God, our Creator. These are 'natural rights' like the right to life or the right to marry. Or they may be based on what are generally accepted among peoples everywhere as reasonable standards of equality, or as appropriate opportunities to achieve this equality. These could be called 'human rights', like the right to own and manage one's own share of property. Although rights like these were recognised long before they were set out in our current universal declarations of human rights, this often went along with significant variations and ambiguities like the acceptance of slavery. Finally, rights may be enshrined in the legislation of a particular State, to safeguard proper equality of these among its people, who are freeborn citizens of that State. These could be called 'civil rights', like the right to a minimum wage, or to certain welfare benefits, or to equal treatment before the law. St Thomas calls these 'positive rights' because they are enshrined in the positive law of the land. Justice conditions us to respect all these various rights, to ensure that everyone is always given his or her due.

INDIVIDUALS, SOCIETY AND THE COMMON GOOD

As the virtue that regulates our relations with other people, justice operates on two levels. On the level of each person's relations with others as individuals, one-to-one, it ensures things like fairness in buying and selling. But it also operates on the level of the relations we have with others simply through belonging to the same society. Anyone who belongs to a given community relates to all those who are included in that community by, for example, paying its taxes, keeping its laws, and so on. Hence justice can affect our relations with other people in either of these two ways: in our one-to-one relationships dealing with each other directly, or in relationships with one another as members of the same society or community.

Anyone who is a member of some community is related to that community as a part is to the whole. Every part of anything belongs, as such, to the whole thing. Whatever is good in any one part can contribute to the good of the whole to which it belongs. So the good represented by the virtue or goodness of any individual in society, whether it perfects that individual within him- or herself or in his or her relations with others, can be directed and contribute to the overall good of the whole community. This overall good is what is generally called 'the common good'. Justice aims to promote and maintain this in society. In this way all activities that are virtuous and good in a society can be brought under the umbrella of justice, as it aims to promote the overall or common good of all that society's members. It is in this sense that justice can be called a general virtue, directing all the other virtues to serve its own purpose. Justice seen in that way is called general justice and sometimes 'legal justice'. This is because it is the function of the law or legal system to direct everything in a society to promoting the common good of that society and of all its members. As its name indicates, the aim of 'legal justice', like the law in any society, is to ensure that the activities of all the citizens serve the common good, or the general wellbeing, of all who belong to that society.

However, even though it directs the practice of all the moral virtues by its citizens to the common good of their society in this way, general justice, is not simply the same thing as all these moral virtues taken together. Aristotle shrewdly remarks: 'Many individuals, who can be quite virtuous in matters concerning themselves, are incapable of being virtuous in matters relating to others ... the virtue of a good individual, then, is not always the same as the virtue of a good citizen'.[6] General justice, which motivates individuals to work for the common good of all their fellow citizens, is thus the distinguishing virtue of good citizens, distinct from their strictly personal virtue or goodness as private individuals. In theory, at least, it is possible to be quite a good private individual, without being a really good citizen. Hence justice keeps its own distinctive identity, while directing all the other moral virtues to work toward its own objective, the common good. It is because it directs the activities of the other virtues to serve its own distinctive goal in this way that legal justice can be described as a general virtue. It marshals the energies of all these other virtues, to ensure that what they prompt people to do, contributes to the common good of all. This is what justice, legal and general, is intended to promote as its own proper goal or objective.

---

6 *Nicomachean Ethics* VI.8; Aquinas, *ST* II.II 50; *Disputed Questions on the Virtues* 1 9-10. An excellent general introduction to Aquinas's views on justice, law and politics is Finnis, *Aquinas: Moral, Political, and Legal Theory* OUP, 1998.

That is why, traditionally, this virtue was said to concern chiefly the rulers of society, as architects of the common good, and only secondarily their subjects, whose place it is to follow the directions of their rulers. In modern democratic societies this idea, that the practice of legal justice to promote the common good of society is primarily the responsibility of governments rather than of those being governed, needs to be heavily qualified. All of us are responsible for creating the kind of just society that caters for the welfare of all its people. We do this by practising that virtue of justice that directs all our efforts to this end. The common good which justice thereby inclines us to promote is the overall good of all of us together, rather than just our own private good as individuals, or as belonging to some particular class or interest group in society.

The tendency to limit concern for this wider area of justice, whether we call it general, legal or social justice, to the ruling classes almost exclusively, may have led in the past to a certain privatisation or individualisation of justice for the rest of us. All we ordinary folk had to be concerned with were our dealings with each other as individuals, one-to-one. So we had to be careful to give each person exactly what was due to him or her in strict justice, paying the exact price for items purchased, giving (and earning) a fair day's pay for a fair day's work, and so on. While this, of course, is an important area for our practice of the virtue of justice, it is not the only, nor even the main concern of justice, as we shall see.

COMMUTATIVE JUSTICE: BETWEEN YOU AND ME

Still this one-to-one kind of justice may well be the first thing that occurs to anyone trying to think of justice as a personal virtue, rather than as a political slogan. So we shall deal with it briefly here. In their Pastoral Letter on *The Work of Justice* in 1977 the Irish Bishops wrote:

> Justice begins with myself and my dealings with others. Justice is about my work, my business, my commercial dealings, my profession, my style of life. Justice is about paying a just and fair wage for a job and doing a just and honest job for the wage. Justice is about buying and selling. It is about employing men and women or making them

redundant. Justice is about meeting my contracts, promising and delivering what I promise at the time promised. Justice is about fair prices and just profits. It is about honesty and truthfulness and straight dealings in work, in business, in public service, in political life.

As already mentioned, justice is designated by a number of specific names to indicate the particular area of human relations with which it is concerned. When it concerns our relations as individuals to the overall common good of our society it is called general, or legal, justice. When it has to do with the relationship of society to its citizens, individually and collectively, it is called distributive justice. When it regulates the relations of individuals to each other in their one-to-one dealings, in transactions such as buying and selling, or work contracts, it is called commutative justice. It gets this name from the fact that it is largely concerned with exchanges between individuals, the Latin word for exchange being *commutare*. This kind of justice inclines me, in my dealings with others, to give each and every individual his or her due or strict rights. This comes into play most typically in exchanges of goods and services between people as, for example, when items of food or clothing are exchanged for their money price, or the work a person does is exchanged for a certain salary or wage. Justice here demands that there should be strict equality between what is given and what is received in return, that is, that one gets value for money (or its equivalent). It is a matter of respecting the other's property and entitlements, of not cheating or stealing from them, of not deliberately damaging what belongs to them, of not withholding from them what is rightly their due.

STEALING, ROBBERY, VANDALISM, FRAUD

Stealing or theft, properly so called, means taking and keeping another person's property against that person's will. It would not really be stealing, then, nor would it go against the proper inclination of justice, if the taker had good reason to believe that the owner would not object to his taking something that belongs to him or her (the owner). There are cases in which it would be unreasonable for the owner to object to his property being taken and used by someone else such as in cases of extreme necessity. So, for example, a man who takes food to keep his family from starving to death, even without the owner's leave, is not guilty of injustice or stealing (though he could be prosecuted under civil law). In such cases of extreme necessity, whatever is necessary and available to sustain or protect people's lives is regarded as the common property of all. Apart from such extreme cases, however, even borrowing another person's property against his or her will is contrary to justice and must be seen as akin to stealing or theft.

Robbery is an aggravated form of theft or stealing. It uses force or violence to deprive the other person of his or her belongings. So it adds assault against the person to the sin of stealing or theft. This is all the more appalling when those who are attacked and robbed in this way are helpless old people, often living alone.

Wilfully to damage the property of other people is also to treat them unjustly. Even to do this unintentionally, through lack of due care, or recklessness, involves an injustice. Justice should incline us to take reasonable care of what belongs to other people whenever we are allowed to use it, or put in charge of it.

Vandalism, or the wanton destruction of even so called public property, cannot be excused of injustice either, on the grounds that the property really belongs to nobody. The frightening increase of this destructive kind of behaviour, especially among young people and even children, should cause us to worry about the state of our society in this matter of justice and respect for what is not one's own. It should also urge us to do what we can to see that conditions that may lead to this kind of anti-social behaviour, like poor housing, or lack of recreational facilities, are removed.

Justice is not only concerned with belongings that can be stolen or robbed or wantonly damaged. It also has to do with the making and keeping of contracts or agreements between people. Justice obliges and inclines us to keep our lawful contracts and avoid all forms of fraud or cheating. So, for example, if you agree to use certain materials in building a house for someone else, you should not substitute cheaper materials and still charge the same price. Neither should you, to purchase something, put yourself in debt, or take out a mortgage which you will not be able to repay.

The contract that concerns most people is of course the 'work contract' between employers and employees. The latter agree to do a certain job, with due diligence and care, in return for an agreed wage, which has to be fair, with proper working conditions. Both sides are obliged and should be urged by justice to keep the terms of this agreement. Issues like wage disputes, pickets, and so on, call for more detailed discussion. Still the basic requirement of justice that we keep our lawful agreements is clear enough.

RIGHT TO LIFE, REPUTATION, PRIVACY, AND SELF-RESPECT

Commutative justice between persons in their exchanges with each other is not just about material goods and belongings, nor only about money, the normal medium of exchange. It is also about respecting more precious commodities, like a person's good name or reputation, bodily integrity and security, and even the basic possession of human life itself. The virtue of justice inclines and requires us always to respect and safeguard each other's rights to these very personal possessions. So it keeps us from injuring other people in any way, in body, mind, or spirit.

The greatest physical injury we could do to anyone would be to kill or murder that person. That is why respect for human life is one of the strongest impulses of the virtue of justice. The few exceptions sometimes discussed, when killing another person would not be wrong, are not likely ever to concern most of us, thank God. These are killing in self-defence, or as a soldier in a war that is justified. There are some people today, however, who want to make even more exceptions, to justify killings that up to now would have been generally regarded as nothing short of murder. These are the people who advocate what is called euthanasia or mercy killing. They would claim that at least in certain cases to kill a person suffering from a very painful terminal illness, or to help that person to die, would not be unjust to that person, since the aim is to put that person out of his or her unbearable misery. There are also those who claim that it is not always wrong or unjust to kill an unborn infant in the womb, by bringing about an abortion. The right of the unborn child to its life is so fundamental that no other right can ever outweigh it. It is equalled only by the right to life of another human being, like that of the child's expectant mother. That is why abortion, as it is widely practised today, must be regarded as a serious injustice against the unborn. The same consideration should rule out euthanasia or mercy killing, in spite of the strong emotion of pity for another's suffering that might push us to condone it.

You do not have to go so far as to kill or murder someone to do them an injustice. It is also unjust deliberately to cause them lesser bodily injuries without sufficient reason. You may, of course, defend yourself when attacked, but you do not have to beat your attacker to a pulp! Injuries caused to other people through our own wilful neglect or carelessness also amount to injustices done to them. The virtue of justice inclines us always to take reasonable care whenever we are doing things that could injure or endanger other people. So it clearly goes against the impulse of justice to drive your car in a condition or in ways or at speeds that endanger other road users and put them at serious risk of injury.

We can also act unjustly towards other people by the way we talk about them. The nursery rhyme that says 'sticks and stones will break my bones, but words can never hurt me', is simply untrue. The worst form of injustice in this regard is called calumny. It means saying things about another person that are not true, with the deliberate intention of injuring that person's good name or reputation, by causing other people to think less of him or her. Neither does the fact that what you say about people is true necessarily save you from being unjust to them. If the faults or misconduct you attribute to someone in this way would otherwise remain hidden and unknown, it may be a case of your being unjust to that person by what is called 'detraction', unless something gives you the right to make their faults known. You could have this right to speak out in order to prevent other people from being injured (for example by a child molester) or to ensure that justice is served in a court of law, or to give someone an honest reference for a job. Otherwise you have no right to let a person's secret faults be known by talking about them. To do so could involve a serious failure in justice, depriving another person of one of his or her most precious possessions, namely his or her good name or reputation.

Another way to injure people by words is to reveal facts about them, even good things, which they want and have a right to keep secret. Just because you find out something about another person you know or suspect they would not generally want to be known, does not give you the right to go and speak about it to others who are not in on the secret. Even prying into other people's secrets, by reading their personal correspondence, or by eavesdropping on private conversations, is a form of injustice done to them.

There are certain secrets which justice binds us even more strictly to keep to ourselves. This is the case with all confidential information entrusted to professionals such as doctors, and lawyers. The only secret that may never be revealed in any circumstances, however, is what the penitent confides to a priest in the sacrament of reconciliation. Other secrets may occasionally have to be divulged for the sake of some greater good, like protecting public safety, health, or security. Short of that, to tell people's secrets is to do them an injustice that could be seriously wrong or sinful Thinking and saying the worst about people, without sufficient grounds, is also to do them an injustice. This is called rash judgement. We all have the right to be considered innocent until our guilt is established, until we are proven guilty, or until there are good enough grounds for concluding that we are.

Finally we can injure other persons with our words by using harsh and abusive language to insult or to make fun of them. Justice inclines us to respect other people's honour and to leave them their self-respect.

RESTITUTION

Whenever we injure another person or persons in their property, person, or good name by the things we deliberately say or do, it is not enough for us just to stop doing these things, to say we are sorry, and that we will not do them again. We have to do what we can to repair any damage we have done to that person, and to make good the loss they have suffered from our actions or neglect. You cannot just hold onto the gains you have made through cheating, or stealing, or dishonest transactions. You have to restore as far as possible these ill-gotten gains to the person or the people to whom they rightly belong. In the same way, you have to try and repair the damage you have done to someone's character or self-respect by careless or malicious words and actions. If you cannot make good the damage itself, than you have to try to compensate the injured party for the damage or loss your injustice has caused them. This is the only way to restore the balance of justice upset by the acts of injustice. That is why it is called restitution. Making restitution is a strict requirement for anyone who wants to be pardoned for sins of injustice that have injured other persons, or deprived them of what was rightly theirs.

In this way the virtue of justice restores and maintains the proper balance between persons in their dealings with each other. It also works to ensure a certain balance among all the persons or sectors that make up society as a whole.

FAIR DISTRIBUTION FOR THE COMMON GOOD OF ALL

We have seen how justice, in its most general application, what Aristotle called the virtue of good citizens, directs the efforts and resources of all its members to bring about the overall good of the society to which they belong. This is the common good of society as distinct from the purely personal or sectional interests of its members. This is what parts of any organism owe to the whole organism of which they are part. This is what is due from them: to be concerned for the overall good of the whole and not just each part 'out' for its own private good. This comes under the general umbrella of justice, which seeks to give all their due, as a requirement of general or legal justice.

There is however another movement of justice in society that goes in the other direction, from society as a whole to its constituent parts or individual members. This is called distributive justice and is concerned with what the whole owes to its parts. Its role is to ensure that the available resources and benefits of a society are fairly distributed amongst all members of that society, so that nobody gets the lion's share of these benefits leaving others to live in want, on the 'poverty line'. This even distribution of the available goods in a society amongst all its members is a matter of justice. People on the receiving end can claim what they receive as their due. Why? Because all the available resources required for happy, healthy living in society are meant to be the common patrimony of all its members. As St Thomas puts it: 'whatever belongs to society as a whole belongs in its own way to each of its parts (or members). So, when the community possessions are distributed among its individual members, each of them is getting only what is his or her own in that sense'.[7]

Obviously it cannot simply be left to individuals to claim what they see as their share of the community's wealth and just take it for themselves and for their families. This would end in chaos. Only those who exercise authority in the community, the government

7 Thomas Aquinas, *Summa theologiae* II.II 61 1 *ad* 2

with its civil service, can make this actual distribution of goods and services to its citizens. They do this, in practice, by providing services for health care, educational facilities, social welfare benefits, and other public services. In their 1977 Pastoral Letter, *The Work of Justice,* the Irish Bishops made the point that the most effective and humane way of distributing wealth in our society is to create employment opportunities for the greatest possible number of its citizens and to reduce unemployment figures to a minimum.

But the fact that this fair distribution of society's wealth amongst its members is mainly the responsibility of the government and its agencies does not mean that they are the only ones who need to practise this virtue of distributive justice. Aquinas says: 'this virtue also belongs to the citizens amongst whom these goods are distributed, in so far as they must consent to their fair distribution' (II.II 61 1 *ad* 3). This is particularly true in a democracy, where rulers are answerable to the people for the decisions they make.

Government's main mechanism for transferring wealth in society from those who have more to those who have less and for financing public services for us all, is the tax system. Justice demands that better-off citizens should be willing to pay higher taxes to improve the lot of the less well-off and to finance the public services required by all. Paying one's taxes is therefore a matter of justice. The Irish Bishop's Pastoral also point out that wage restraint on the part of people in secure employment can also be a requirement of justice towards others who are jobless, or who suffer from greater job insecurity. Excessive demands for higher living standards can obstruct the creation of new jobs and can threaten existing jobs.

All these things then are matters for the virtue of distributive justice, as it seeks to spread the benefits of our society more evenly among its members. Though complete equality may never be achieved, and might not even be desirable, justice will not allow us to let the poor get poorer while the rich get richer, be it in our own society or the wider world community. This is particularly the case for Christian believers, in whom God's gift of grace, through faith, hope and charity, opens the virtue of justice to the Holy Spirit's gift of piety. This gift of the Spirit makes us ready and eager not only to honour and respect God as our Father, but also to respect all human beings as God's own children, our sisters and brothers in Jesus Christ.

XIII

The Blessing of Law

JOSEPH KAVANAGH, OP

THE BLESSING OF LAW

Joseph Kavanagh, OP

'there is nothing given that cannot be reimagined'
– Seamus Heaney, *The Settle Bed*

INTRODUCTION

The reflections in this article, whatever their worth, owe much to my being designated, as a young Dominican, to do postgraduate studies in canon law, and later, to teach in the regional seminary of Trinidad & Tobago. Neither posting was my choice – indeed both came as a shock to the system! – but hindsight particularly allows me to view them as singular blessings. Hence the readiness with which I accepted the invitation to write on this topic, for both in Rome and the Caribbean I was made to struggle with the idea – and the practice – of law within the Christian community. I make no claim to academic insight: these lines are random thoughts, rather, that flit like butterflies in and out of memory.

Rome is the ancient matrix of a whole culture of law, yet nowhere have I experienced law to sit so lightly on people's shoulders. Maybe this should not be surprising, since those for whom law is so embedded in their psyche have surely come to know its place and acknowledge its wider social significance. Be that as it may, the timing and placing of my assignation to study canon law were to prove significant for me. It was 1964, and the text of the 1918 Code of Canon Law was already under revision. This body of law, which had been so fixed, was questionable suddenly, and its aura of permanence was – for better or for worse – stripped away. And the men (no women as yet!) who formed the faculty of canon law in the 'Angelicum' [Pontifical University of St Thomas Aquinas, Rome] were a lively and likeable group who kept pushing us back into the philosophical underpinning of the various texts. It did not make for easy going, but it kept us aware of the place of law in the wider context of faith and ideas.

When on completion of my studies and my stint in Rome I was assigned to the church in Trinidad & Tobago, I was catapulted into a society that was experiencing social upheaval and revolt. It was 1970, and the black power movement of North America had spilled over into its southern neighbours, provoking a flurry of self-analysis and lively debate throughout the region. Some of the most radical black thinking was taking place in the seminary, and it was into the highly-charged atmosphere of this place that I was asked to go with my white skin and my canon law. It is not hard to imagine how quickly and fiercely Caribbean hackles rose in the face of my colonial baggage – and how I came to avoid carefully any early canonical discourse on the fittingness of '*obsequium*' or any other such refined matters! Indeed, my baptism of fire had been occasioned by the hasty removal of my (European) predecessor, whose version of canon law nearly precipitated a riot in the seminary. This heady context drove me back to the wisdom of my Angelicum professors, in search of a rationale for canon law in a very different – and revolutionary – society. What I came to appreciate – in the face of my critical students – was that there truly is a place for law in every human context, and within that place it is most assuredly a blessing.

MEMORY THAT ENABLES

Mary Grey[1] decries the 'structured amnesia' that is at the root of so much injustice and oppression. This is certainly the case when we turn our attention to the culture of law within the Church. Not that lawyers are noted for forgetfulness – far from it! – but that in the transmission of the wisdom of our ancestors there is a tendency towards a certain diminishment or even erosion of elements that other times and situations deemed essential to the concept and practice of law. I think of the force of custom, the significance of reception, the role of *epikeia* and equity in the field of jurisprudence, and the supremacy of conscience, to name some of the more obvious.

1. Emeritus Professor of Theology, University of Wales, Lampeter and Visiting Professor, St Mary's College, Strawberry Hill, Twickenham, London, Mary's research has focused primarily on feminist liberation theology and spiritualities, and she has written on ecofeminist theology and globalisation.

I believe these critical areas have been either sidelined in practice or corralled by professionals, both in the teaching of canon law and in its application. Yves Congar's famous and painful thesis that one of the root causes of atheism in Europe today is a complacent church and an uncritical ecclesiology[2] is paralleled by the disservice done to law by an approach that spares no time for these fundamental and necessarily elusive elements, but that rushes immediately to the deceptive certainties of text. Thus, ecclesiastical scribalism is born, the text invested with inflated status and unquestioned authority, to the detriment of law's proper interaction in the life of the church. At root there is here a kind of laziness, when answers are sought simply in the formula of the law, as though the lawmaker's role is to provide solutions and dispense the community and the individual from wrestling with the complexities of their world.

Paul VI was acutely aware of this danger, as we shall see in his insistence on the constant correction of equity. But too easily the urge for clear answers turns exclusively – and pathologically – to the text, and away from the complex demands of a more complete response. And we have all been responsible for this: legislators who appropriate exclusively the right to interpret laws, and all of us who abdicate responsibility for wrestling with the demands of each situation. Memory is called for, to re-collect the factors that save us from the tyranny of the text, and help shape a response that is wholesome and human. Dermot Lane's words from another context are relevant here: 'Memory enables people to realise that the way we are is not the way we have to be, and in this regard memory has the power to activate a new praxis'.[3]

There is a need to restore critical memory to its place at a time such as this when the Church is struggling to realise the ecclesiology of Vatican II. The late John Paul II's open invitation to dialogue about the shape of the emerging Church reminds us that this is not just a domestic matter for the church of Rome but for the whole

2 Congar, Yves, 'Une conclusion théologique a l'enquête sur les raisons actuelles de l'incroyance' (A theological conclusion to the survey of the current reasons for unbelief), *La Vie Intellectuelle*, VI (1935) 214-49

3 Lane, Dermot, *Keeping Hope Alive – Stirrings in Christian Theology*, Dublin 1996, Gill & Macmillan, 202

Christian family. The Polish Pontiff's invitation gives particular focus to the plurality of traditions, and it is no coincidence that subsequent ecumenical discussion has chosen to bring to this plurality the ancient canonical concept of reception. It was Congar who made this connection with reception[4], but its precedents are really canonical, and its roots deep.

DIVERSITY THAT CHALLENGES

I have never been to the Rupununi, an area of the interior of Guyana that reaches down to the Amazon. People describe it as another world, remote and cut off from the rest of Guyana – and the rest of human society! But the church is there, and one of the students in my canon law class was from there. I wondered about him, heading back to his people with passes in his canon law exams, and hoped he would quickly forget the intricacies of canonical annulment rather than our (betimes confused!) classroom debate on the reception of law. Indeed, this is a topic that calls out for attention as the Church seeks to be meaningfully realised in a world of bewildering diversity and inequality. If canon law is to be a blessing for the people of Rupununi, then for them it has to mirror both the challenge and the respect of the gospel. Thus it needs, not just to be carefully formulated, but to honour the diverseness of local situations and cultures and be received by those who are uniquely able to understand what the legislator cannot be expected to know.

The roots of this concept of reception go back to medieval times, and specifically to the *Decretum* of Gratian. When this 12th century monk wrote his famous dictum, 'laws are instituted when promulgated; confirmed when approved by the users' (*leges instituuntur, cum promulgantur, firmantur, cum moribus utentium approbantur*, D.4, C.3), and thereby formulated the teaching on the reception of law, it is important to appreciate that he did so in a discussion of the law's intrinsic finality and nature. He was not

---

4 Congar, Yves, 'La réception comme réalité ecclésiologique', *Revue des Sciences Philosophiques et Théologiques 56* (1972), 370. 'By "reception" I understand the process by which an ecclesial body truly makes its own a resolution which it had not given to itself, recognising in the measure so promulgated a rule which is applicable to its own life.'

considering or questioning the authority of the lawmaker, or even, for that matter, the possibility of conflict between the legislator and a particular community. Indeed, it is possible, in his view, for a community to decide that a particular law does not apply in their case without thereby diminishing in any way the authority of the lawmaker. Once formulated, all laws embody qualities that are consonant with the common good – as perceived by 'right reason' and famously outlined by the pseudo-Isidore[5] – failing which even the most exalted legislative authority cannot validate them.

This understanding of reception makes eminent sense within the Thomistic tradition of law, which sees the law's authority rooted in its link with, and effective fostering of, the common good of the community. But it is not hard to understand why it has, so to speak, slipped off the screen. In a church administration which, particularly since the rejection of conciliarism in the late eighteenth century, has effectively espoused a voluntarist understanding of law – sourcing the authority of law in the will of the legislator – the teaching of reception is only too easily dismissed as fostering anarchy, or else is hedged in with caveats about capriciousness and arbitrary choices. And the *stilus* of the church administration in the past thirty years suggests that this voluntarism is still very healthy and robust!

For all that, there are indications that the time is ripe for a return to centre stage of Aquinas' teaching on the common good basis of all authentic law, and with this, a recovery of the place of reception in the life of the church. The past fifty years have witnessed a remarkable retrieval of the virtue-centred moral philosophy of Aquinas (as distinct from the prevailing law-centred approach), which augurs well for a long-overdue return to a Thomist conception of law. The Second Vatican Council, and the subsequent Code of Canon Law, support this trend.

When the present Code was promulgated in 1983, the introductory Apostolic Constitution of John Paul II was emphatic

---

5 'Law will be upright, just, possible, in accord with nature and the customs of the country, suitable to place and time, necessary, useful, clear insofar as it does not through obscurity contain something unsuitable, not for private benefit, but for the common wellbeing of the general public' – *Decretum Gratiani*, D. 4, C.2

about the importance of relating the new legal text to the image of the Church of Vatican II as to its primary pattern, speaking of 'the fundamental basis of newness which ... is found in ... (the Council's) ecclesiological teaching'. This echoed Paul VI's leitmotiv of the need for a new mindset (*novus habitus mentis*) in approaching the Church's legislation in the aftermath of the Council. Most significant here – in the context of the need for a recovery of reception in the life of the community – is the Council's call for the Church to model itself on the biblical image of a people on pilgrimage together, with all this image's overtones of responsibility and trust. The implications of this are considerable, not least for the acceptance of subsidiarity as a keystone of church administration, and a radical revision of the manner of episcopal appointment. The autocratic ruler belongs to another time, is anachronistic, and most importantly, is alien to the spirit of the gospel.

When I think of my student now, working among his people, I have no qualms about the class hours spent on the subtleties of canonical annulment procedures. He knows well enough these have their place and that they do not impinge on the realities of his people – they simply have never been received in Rupununi. And that is all right. There are no sleepless nights in the Congregation of the Sacraments over this – and for the remote Amazonian communities, the ancient wisdom of reception is accepted. This instance has many parallels, not all of them nearly so geographically remote, and they suggest we lift up our European gaze to acknowledge that Isidore and Gratian and Thomas – and, indeed, Aristotle - have much to tell us from their wisdom.

RESTRAINTS THAT HUMBLE

'Short laws, good laws' – this was an aphorism much favoured by one of our Angelicum professors. Initially we thought that it was his playful way of suggesting that short laws gave commentators like himself more scope to wander all over the place. But we were to learn that in fact it came from his conviction that the wise legislator does not attempt to make the formulation of the law cover every conceivable situation, dreaming of a 'misplaced concreteness'.[6] Indeed once words are carved out – however carefully and painstakingly – they bring to the final product their intrinsic limits and cultural restrictions. And between the law and the action there is a process in which the law's *ordinatio* interacts with other factors to help bring about a prudential decision. It is a disservice to the law to see it simply as a solution to be slapped on a particular situation – yet, surprising as it may seem, this is frequently the very way law is treated. It is, moreover, a disservice to the dignity and responsibility of the human person when unquestioning adherence to the law is demanded, ascribing an unwarranted absoluteness to the law's formulation. No one was more conscious of the law's inherent limitations than Aquinas (cf. *Summa theologiae* I-II 91, 3 *ad* 3), who stated that even the written text of the gospels by itself kills (I-II 106, 2) – *a fortiori* the written formula of the human lawmaker.

All of this may seem so obvious, yet the ancient *juris prudentes* saw fit to introduce checks and balances to the seemingly inherent human tendency to inflate the law beyond its basic helpful role. Among these we may single out the practice of equity. This concept came into medieval jurisprudence through the Code of Justinian, as a way of safeguarding the community from a rigid and unyielding administration of the law and ensuring that 'the rigour of the law [be] tempered by the sweetness of mercy' (Henry of Susa, 1271). In recent times, it was Paul VI who, more than anyone, kept recalling church administrators to medieval teaching: '[it] represents one of the highest aspirations of mankind. If social life makes the laying down of human laws necessary, nevertheless their guidelines – inevitably general and abstract – cannot foresee the concrete circumstances in which the law will be applied. Faced with this problem, canon law has sought to amend, rectify and even correct the *rigor iuris*, and this is brought about through equity, which thus turns these human aspirations in the direction of a higher kind of justice' (*Acta Apostolicae Sedis* LXV [1973] 95).

6 Bishop, Jordan, 'Natural Law and Ethics: some second thoughts', *New Blackfriars*, vol. 77, n. 907 (1996), 386

And if equity acknowledges the limitations of law in the social forum, there is its counterpart in the inner forum of conscience, *epikeia*, another wise constraining element drawn this time from Plato and Aristotle. Within the church tradition, epikeia is understood to have its proper place in the personal forum of conscience, whereby an individual considers that she/he is excused from the observance of the law in a particular instance. Aquinas places it within the virtue of justice, and sees, as its function, to bypass a law that is judged to be deficient, i.e., 'instead of being just and useful, it is in fact useless and even unjust.'[7]

Intimately linked with both equity and *epikeia* is the critical field of conscience, an area that is anathema to the despot and the tyrant, be they captain of a golf club, leader of a nation, or priest in his parish. In Christian tradition, martyrs are the great witnesses to conscience, but there are countless instances in all areas of daily life when this vital factor comes into play. It is the final and inviolable block to tyranny in all its forms, and has always been held in special esteem down through the Church's life. Enough here though to recall the strong words of the present Pope, written in 1968, commenting on the Second Vatican Council's Document on The Church in the Modern World, *Gaudium et spes*:

> Over the pope as the expression of the binding claim of ecclesiastical authority, there still stands one's own conscience, which must be obeyed before all else, if necessary even against the requirement of ecclesiastical authority. This emphasis on the individual, whose conscience confronts him with a supreme and ultimate tribunal, and one which in the last resort is beyond the claim of external social groups, even of the official Church, also establishes a principle in opposition to increasing totalitarianism.[8]

It is surely not too fanciful to understand these words being rooted in the young Josef Ratzinger's experience of Hitler's regime

---

7 Fanfani, L. J., OP, *Manuale theorico-practicum theologiae moralis ad mentem D. Thomae*, I, Rome 1950, 197. See *Summa theologiae* II-II 120, 1

8 Vorgrimler, Herbert, ed., *Commentary on the Documents of Vatican II*, London 1968: Burns & Oates, 134

in wartime Germany. They are certainly timely today, when all kinds of global forces conspire to diminish the precious freedom of the individual and override the cultural heritage of local traditions.

HUMOUR THAT LIBERATES

Law is serious. It has an aura of heavy sobriety. And people who dispense the law tend to be somewhat like the Little Prince's red-faced gentleman, 'who has never smelled a flower, never looked at a star'. Which makes it all the more urgent that a conscious effort be made to bring to it that most valuable human attribute of humour. The ancients linked worship, *latria*, and play, *eutrapelia*, to remind us of the need to hold important things lightly, and it was a feature of our best canon law teachers that they brought a dimension of lightness, even irreverence, to their topic. In this they dispensed an unforgettable lesson, and reflected the medieval tradition of the 'feast of fools' – a practice that brought play into the most serious arenas and pricked the pompousness of many events and personages. Here too I learned from my time in Trinidad, with its annual incredible carnival and particularly its '*ole mas*', where fun was poked at everything and from which no one was exempt. I cannot help imagining carnival come to St Peter's Square, and members of the Sacred Roman Rota all dancing in gay abandon – even for a day. Somehow I think it would do more for the furtherance of the gospel than does an unremitting gravity.

I opened these few thoughts with a line from the poet Seamus Heaney. Bequeathed a settle bed by an old neighbour, this gift became for him a metaphor of his Irish world, with its tribal taboos and religious constraints. The 'un-get-roundable weight' of the bed, however, is transformed by the poet's imagination, and he discovers through it a world of dreams, where daring possibilities and exciting vistas open up, not least that of a playful neighbour-God, who bequeaths a whole dower of settle beds from heaven:

... But to conquer that weight,

Imagine a dower of settle beds tumbled from heaven
Like some nonsensical vengeance come on the people,
Then learn from that harmless barrage that whatever is given

Can always be re-imagined, however four-square,
Plank-thick, hull-stupid and out of its time
It happens to be. You are free as the lookout

That far-seeing joker posted high over the fog
Who declared by the time that he had got himself down
The actual ship had been stolen away from beneath him[9].

At the end of the day, we will be best served in our approach to law – and life – if we remember to honour the 'far-seeing joker' within ourselves.

9 Heaney, Seamus, 'The Settle Bed', in *Seeing Things*, London 1991, Faber & Faber

XIV

Companions or Opponents:
The Challenge of Church-State Relations

JOHN HARRIS, OP

COMPANIONS OR OPPONENTS:
THE CHALLENGE OF CHURCH-STATE RELATIONS

John Harris, OP

Pondering the meaning of democracy, C.S. Lewis, a committed Christian and insightful observer of social trends and their inherent risks, had this to say: 'Nor of course must they ever be allowed to raise Aristotle's question: whether "democratic behaviour" means the behaviour that democracies like or the behaviour that will preserve a democracy. For if they did, it could hardly fail to occur to them that these need not be the same.'[1]

If Lewis is correct, then one has to ask some very fundamental questions about what exactly democracy is; and, if indeed it is a value to be preserved, how is it best made secure? Pope John Paul II believed that Christianity could play a vital role in the defence and promotion of 'authentic democracy'. As the third Christian millennium begins, many in Ireland reject outright the belief that the Church can have a positive role to play in the political life of the State. There seems to be little awareness that Christianity can enhance and support democratic ideals. It is taken for granted that democracy can flourish only in an atmosphere of moral relativism or agnosticism[2]. Any attempt to introduce questions of morality is seen as divisive in democratic debate. Having religious beliefs is tantamount to being termed a religious fundamentalist, and any acceptance of the ethical dignity of the State is 'anathema'. Religion is viewed, at best, as a private matter and, at worst, a cause of division and alienation.Can such an impression be left unchallenged by Christians?

In his book *The End of Irish Catholicism*, Vincent Twomey makes the case that the prevalent political culture, or as he calls it 'the new State religion of modern Ireland', is one of 'fundamentalist

---

1 C.S. Lewis, *The Screwtape Letters* (with *Screwtape Proposes a Toast*) revised edition. The definitive edition, containing the C.S. Lewis Preface of 1960, *Screwtape Proposes a Toast* New York, Collier Books. Macmillan Publishing Company, 1961. Copyright 1982, pp. 161-162

2 John Paul II, *Centesimus annus*, n° 46

individualism' or 'fundamentalist secularism', 'where self-interest is the great modern motivating principle – and all in the name of personal liberty and emancipation'.[3] In this vision of political life, the world of religion, and in particular the Catholic Church, is looked upon with suspicion. In the past the Catholic Church in Ireland was not very accepting of those who disagreed with it, and this modern approach may partly be in response to that. But, in the interests of Irish society, each side needs to re-examine the other's position. Regretting this out-lawing of religion from public policy, Gerry Whyte says, firstly, that 'it restricts freedom of expression for religious believers, privileging secular convictions and generating the same feelings of resentment for believers as non-believers experience in religiously monist societies. Secondly, it deprives society of the benefit of religiously inspired values'.[4]

With the Second Vatican Council the Church began a re-examination of her stance regarding Church-State relations. Rather than the Church promoting her own position or influence in the State, this renewed theology (further developed during the papacy of John Paul II) calls upon the Church to interact with political institutions in the interest of the human person's true dignity and the well-being of 'authentic democracy'.

ALL SYSTEMS UPHOLD MORAL VALUES

It is not my intent here to deal with the influence of religion in society in general terms, nor indeed in terms of a particular religious denomination's influence on a culture or people, but rather to look at 'religiously inspired values' which can be of benefit to society. If one were to remove the word *religion* and replace it with the word *morality* or *moral dimension*, then the context of the debate would become clearer. To accept that there is a moral dimension in the area of politics is simply to say that 'every institution, every law and policy, every decision and action which the State performs … shapes and moulds human life in a certain way, by both suggesting and offering certain values as important, and imposing them on

3 Vincent Twomey, *The End of Irish Catholicism* Dublin, Veritas Publications, 2003, p. 114, together with footnote 5

4 Gerry Whyte, Introduction, in Bernard Treacy and Gerry Whyte, editors, *Religion, Morality and Public Policy* Dublin, Dominican Publications, 1995, p. 8

us. It is, in short, a very definite system of moral formation and education'.[5]

Thus, when we speak of morality's influence on the State, we are discussing which virtues fundamentally shape our life in community. Even the notion of tolerance is a regulatory virtue, which will shape the kind of society one lives in. One then needs to ask *how* tolerant will our tolerance be. The question thus is not whether or not a system has a morality: but rather, which one.

Pope John Paul II feared that the moral ethic of western democracies was that of ethical relativism. 'There are those who consider such relativism an essential condition of democracy, inasmuch as it alone is held to guarantee tolerance, mutual respect between people and acceptance of the decisions of the majority, whereas moral norms considered to be objective and binding are held to lead to authoritarianism and intolerance'.[6] In the interest of one's own absolute freedom one must also allow such freedom to others. Therefore tolerance becomes the single most important social virtue. Within this perspective the introduction of the question of morality is seen as a threat to one's freedom and must therefore be expelled from the public arena. 'A seeming[ly] inevitable consequence of this development is the erection of a *cordon sanitaire* around religious convictions when one comes to debate matters of public policy'.[7] The State is called upon therefore to defend the absolute right to freedom and promote tolerance and respect for all opinions. It is the State's role to provide the largest possible arena of freedom to its citizens, so that they can live out their individual choices[8].

But for John Paul II such an understanding runs the risk of destroying democracy itself. According to the Pope the moral value of democracy is not automatic. It depends on conformity to the moral law to which, it 'like every form of human behaviour, must be subject: in other words, its morality depends on the morality of

---

5 Fergal O'Connor, 'Church and State', *The Furrow 30* (1979) p. 279

6 John Paul II, *Evangelium vitae*, n° 70

7 Gerry Whyte, Introduction, in Bernard Treacy and Gerry Whyte, editors, *Religion, Morality and Public Policy* Dublin, Dominican Publications, 1995, p. 8

8 *cf.* John Paul II, *Evangelium vitae*, n° 69

the ends which it pursues and of the means which it employs'.[9] When democracy is misunderstood as the purely formal rule of the majority, it has no objective moral anchor and readily 'moves toward a form of totalitarianism'.[10] The Pope developed this idea while addressing a group of U.S. Bishops at their *ad limina* visit in 1998: 'If there is no objective standard to help adjudicate between different conceptions of the personal and common good, then democratic politics is reduced to a raw contest for power. If constitutional and statutory laws are not held accountable to the objective moral law, the first casualties are justice and equity, for they become matters of personal opinion'.[11]

THE SOTERIOLOGY OF THE STATE
VS. THE MORAL AGNOSTICISM OF THE STATE

What values we uphold are radically influenced by our idea of what we want from the State. Is the State to be 'Big Brother', involved in every aspect of the citizens' lives, or is it simply a disinterested facilitator of social organisation? We have seen in the history of Europe over the last century how the role of the State has taken on a precedence over the rights of its citizens. This has happened both on the left of the political spectrum in Communism and on the right in Fascism. Partly in reaction to this, since the end of World War Two, the opposite approach has become the accepted political ideal in many societies, and we have entered into what is commonly called 'the age of post modernism'. The rights of the individual have been given absolute priority over any consideration of the common good. The State is seen simply as the guarantor of individual rights.

Paradoxically, hand-in-hand with the growth of exaggerated individualism is the growing power of the State and its involvement in the lives of its citizens. In the name of greater security, or economic development, citizens allow the apparatus of the State to curtail civil liberties or direct their lives. This is seen as governments take over more and more the running of social services, schools, hospitals, etc. Governments dictate what subjects

---

9 *Evangelium vitae,* n° 70,4
10 *op. cit.,* n° 20,2
11 *Origins,* 28:16 (1998), p. 284

are to be taught in schools and colleges and what medical care is to be provided in hospitals. There are now government departments for child-care, women's issues, culture, sport, and so on. Areas that a number of years ago would have been considered outside the concern of the State apparatus are now considered as being integral to a government's organisation.

The soteriology of the State (a secular form of salvation which, like all idolatries, ends in destruction) and a moral agnosticism of the State (an illusory 'freedom without truth') are two false political solutions to problems of coordination. If culture and society are to be protected from these, then another way has to be found.

WHAT THE CHURCH HAS TO OFFER

For the Church, any true understanding of society must be built upon a true understanding of the human person, and ultimately on his or her relationship with God. The human person cannot be understood without God, and society cannot be appreciated without first of all acknowledging the truth of humanity[12]. The human person as the *imago Dei*, a child of God, with an openness to relationship with God, must be at the root of any true ethic of society. The attempt to build society on any other foundation, or to describe society in any other terms, will lead to a false anthropology and thus to social disintegration. The Church therefore invites all people and social institutions to measure their judgements and decisions against the values of the gospel, which contain within them the inspired truth about God and humanity[13]. As the Second Vatican Council said, it is the Church's belief that there can be no true understanding of the human person apart from the mystery of God, and ultimately it is in the mystery of the Incarnation that the truth of humanity is revealed[14]. Indeed if the human can be adequately comprehended without reference to Christ then the Church has nothing to offer. For the Christian, humanity's horizons are not bound only by the temporal order, nor regulated solely by social efficiency and political pragmatism. We have an eternal destiny, and it is this dimension which the Church must continue

12 *Gaudium et spes*, n°12
13 *Catechism of the Catholic Church*, n° 2244
14 *Gaudium et spes*, n° 22

to keep before the mind of the world[15]. This transcendent mystery which lies at the heart of each human being gives direction to the building of a true and just society. Built on this true understanding the State can then organize itself in the interest of the citizen and his or her flourishing.

SOCIETY BUILT ON A SOLID MORAL FOUNDATION

Each human being, made in the image of God, lives in society, and his or her social reality is part of their coming to a true understanding of themselves. Since both the Church and civil society are interested in the flourishing of the human person, they share a common project. While their perspectives are distinct, the one secular, the other religious, they are not separate, since they meet in their common concern for the good of the individual. In this common bond are rooted the Church's social commitment and her openness to society. Her interest in the good of society is rooted in her belief that she, as the sacrament of salvation for the human family[16], has an understanding of the person and therefore of society distinct from all other interested parties. Therefore she must speak to the problems and concerns of society bringing to them the light of the gospel. The Church's mission is a religious one, and she willingly admits that she has nothing else to offer society.

As far as the Church is concerned, it is when the State accepts the wonder of the creation of the individual and his or her call to a life lived in God, that the State can best fulfil its mission. While the State can be aware of this reality it is not the role of the State to make sure that this relationship with God is advanced. Given that the State has its own specific secular character, that it is not the sacrament of salvation, its specific interest is the protection and promotion of peace and justice within society. Within this secure environment the human person is free to discover the truth for himself or herself. Nonetheless, the State cannot be unaware of the truths of the human person, since its own survival depends upon these being respected. Freedom without truth leads to destruction. Without obedience to the transcendent truth, which allows us to achieve our full identity, there is no way of ensuring the just

15 *Gaudium et spes*, n° 76
16 *op. cit.*, n° 41

relations between people that prevent society becoming an arena of competing power blocks[17]. As Pope Benedict XVI has reminded the political world; 'a healthy secularism of the State, by virtue of which temporal realities are governed according to their own norms but which does not exclude those ethical references that are ultimately founded in religion, is legitimate. The autonomy of the temporal sphere does not exclude close harmony with the superior and complex requirements that derive from an integral vision of man and his eternal destiny'.[18]

There are certain meta-juridical questions which all societies have to face openly and honestly. These questions concern the very concept of society itself, as a human construct, or as a given. Is society founded on some social contract in which people pool their individual liberties in their own interests? Or is society part of the way in which we achieve our full human fulfilment and true human subjectivity? Western society has, over the years, made certain fundamental choices about the establishment of liberal democracies, by affirming the transcendent dignity of the human person, the role of reason and freedom, the distinction between the religious and secular spheres, and the separation of powers within a constitutional framework. There is no doubt that this development has grown out of a Christian heritage. The question now needs to be asked: can such democracies continue to sustain themselves when cut off from their Christian roots? In the mind of Vatican II no human law is as powerful as the gospel in safeguarding the personal dignity and freedom of the human being in the pursuit of truth[19].

IN PARTNERSHIP FOR A TRULY HUMAN SOCIETY

The claim that the gospel is a support to true understanding of the State is not an attempt to establish a theocracy. Rather, such a claim aims at supporting the belief and affirmation of the fundamental dignity of the person in which are rooted human rights, and upon which any true State must be founded. 'It is the Church's role to remind men of good will of these rights and to

17 John Paul II, *Centesimus annus*, n° 44
18 Benedict XVI, Address to the President of the Italian Republic, 24 June 2005 in *L'Osservatore Romano* (English edition), N. 26 (1900), 29 June 2005, p. 3
19 *Gaudium et spes*, n° 41

distinguish them from unwarranted or false claims'.[20] This is not about establishing the Holy Roman Empire once more, but is an attempt to make sure that never again will our world know the scourges of Communism or Fascism. 'Totalitarianism arises out of a denial of truth in the objective sense. If there is no transcendent truth, in obedience to which man achieves his full identity, then there can be no sure principle of guaranteeing just relations between people'.[21] The Church's only concern is for the true development of each person, and this can be best cared for by acknowledging that we are not our own creation but that, as part of creation, part of the eternal plan, we come to our true selves. When the Church asks to be listened to, it is not out of some longing for political power or influence, but rather in the interest of defending and promoting the dignity of the human person.

This teaching is not a specifically *religious* truth and so to be rejected by those who are non-religious. It is the truth which all right-minded people can appreciate. Because there is an intrinsic connection between the dignity of the human person and the Church's social doctrine, the Church's position can be appreciated by those who are not Church members. The grounding of the Church's social doctrine in the dignity of the human person allows the Church to enter common cause, for the good of humanity, with people of other faiths and those who claim to have no religious beliefs. What better proof can the Church offer that she no longer desires a confessional State? She is willing to accept the insights of those who are not Catholic and, together with them, build an authentic society based on the truth of human dignity.

The Church sees herself as working with all people of good will to build a true society. She asks that people accept her intentions as honourable. In the interest of building an earthly city that is truly human she offers to all those of good will the insights that she has received from attending, for 2,000 years, at the school of her Lord and Master. In this involvement in society the Church asks that truths should not be excluded from the political arena, just because they are also considered religious truths. A viewpoint should not be

---

20 *Catechism of the Catholic Church,* n° 1930
21 John Paul II, *Veritatis splendor,* n° 99

excluded from public debate simply because it is held on religious grounds, if it can be proven that it serves the integral promotion of the person and of society. To exclude a view simply because it is held on religious grounds is to be guilty of a form of intolerant secularism. 'Such a position would seek to deny not only the engagement of Christianity in public or political life, but even the possibility of natural ethics itself. Were this the case, the road would be open to moral anarchy, which would be anything but legitimate pluralism'.[22]

The Church believes that she has something to offer society, while acknowledging that civil society has its own autonomous sphere of influence. She believes that 'her vision of the dignity of the person revealed in all its fullness in the mystery of the Incarnate Word'[23] allows her to inform society as to the true ethical dignity of the State. The Church believes that she can speak to every person of good will, for she speaks not only from the source of revelation but also from the common natural law, which lies in the heart of each of us.

VICTIM OF HER HISTORY

The Church, however, realises that in the past her intentions in the political sphere were not always pure. The Church has used her position in society to gain political power and influence. In the Second Vatican Council's *Declaration on Religious Freedom* the Church admits that at times the Church acted in ways 'hardly in keeping with the Gospel and even opposed to it'.[24] During the Holy Year of 2000 Pope John Paul II led the entire Church in a public act of repentance asking the Lord's forgiveness for the sins, past and present, of the Church's sons and daughters. On that day the Pope prayed for forgiveness for the sins committed in the service of the truth. The Pope prayed: 'Lord, God of all men and women, in certain periods of history Christians have at times given in to intolerance and have not been faithful to the great commandment of love, sullying in this way the face of the Church, your Spouse. Have mercy on your sinful children, and accept our resolve to seek and

22 Congregation for the Doctrine of the Faith, *Doctrinal Note on some Questions regarding the Participation of Catholics in Political Life*, Vatican City, Libreria Editrice Vaticana, 2002, pp. 20-21, n° 6.5

23 John Paul II, *Centesimus annus*, n° 47

24 *Dignitatis humanae*, n° 12

promote truth in the gentleness of charity, in the firm knowledge that truth can prevail only in virtue of truth itself'.[25]

The Church now asks the political community to accept her resolve to be of service to the true dignity of the human person and thus of society. The Church sees herself, not being motivated by worldly ambition but as endeavouring to carry on the work of Christ under the guidance of the Holy Spirit[26]. She asks all who are involved in political activity to recognise this statement for what it truly is and to accept that it is spoken out of authentic concern for the good of the person in society and not out of some desire for political influence. John Paul II, speaking to European society, said: 'Do not be afraid! The Gospel is not against you but for you... Be confident! In the Gospel, which is Jesus, you will find the sure and lasting hope to which you aspire'.[27]

The reason for an anti-religious bias may have its intellectual roots in the Enlightenment and the desire for absolute freedom for the individual, God being seen as placing intolerable limits on such freedom. But it may also be the result of the experience of the Irish Church. If this is so, then development is asked for on both sides of the debate. The Church needs to be more forthcoming in her renewed theology of Church-State issues; and those on the other side of the debate must become more open, so as to accept that the Church's attitude to society has developed. The example of John Paul II's prayer for forgiveness may be a means by which the Irish Church could look at herself and see the ways in which she has at times given in to intolerance and not been faithful to the great commandment of love. Perhaps she needs to resolve to seek and promote truth in the gentleness of charity, in the firm knowledge that truth can prevail only in virtue of truth itself.

A PLURALIST SOLUTION

The Church in Ireland, while recognising her past sins, must yet endeavour to introduce her present position to those who fear her. With the confidence of John Paul II, she must say that public

25   http://www.vatican.va/news_services/liturg.../ns_lit_doc_20000312_prayer-day-pardon_en.htm

26 *Gaudium et spes*, n° 3

27 John Paul II, Post-Synodal Apostolic Exhortation *Ecclesia in Europa*, Vatican City, Libreria Editrice Vaticana, 2003, n° 121

life has nothing to fear in the Gospel regarding the proper organisation of society. The Church must say to those who fear her that for her too it is the dignity of the human person that is her central concern in social matters. When the Church proclaims God's gift of salvation, she contributes to the enrichment of human dignity[28]. The truth needs to be preached so as to be seen for its authenticity, as the way to true freedom. 'In a world without the truth freedom loses its foundation and man is exposed to the violence of passion and to manipulation'.[29] The Church must build bridges within society with other social partners in their common care for individual human rights. This may take time, it may involve a time of healing of past hurts and the removal of the fear of domination. The Council reminds us it may take 'a considerable time to arrive at the desired goal' in order to bring people who are perhaps estranged 'into harmony with spiritual realities'.[30] Aquinas teaches that law must lead gently, encourage, rather than be forceful and cause harm[31]. In her preaching of the Gospel in Irish society, the Church needs to reach beyond past hurts, and be mindful of others' concerns as well as their ability or inability to listen.

But this must not silence her, for to remain silent would be to turn her back on the world and refuse to be the sacrament of the Risen Lord. All the Church asks is to be allowed to take part in the debate and have her opinion taken seriously. It must not be cast aside simply because it is the Church's position. The Church, as we have seen, believes that her ethical position vis-à-vis the ordering of political life is rooted in human nature itself and belongs to the natural moral law. 'The challenges facing a democratic State demand from all men and women of good will, irrespective of their particular persuasion, supportive and generous cooperation in the building up the common good of the Nation. Such cooperation, however, cannot prescind from reference to the fundamental ethical values inscribed in the very nature of the human person'.[32]

28 John Paul II, *Centesimus annus*, n° 55

29 *ibid.*, n° 46

30 *Gaudium et spes*, n° 29

31 *Summa theologiae* I.II 96 2 *ad* 2

32 John Paul II's address to the Italian Parliament, 14 November 2002, n° 5 *L'Osservatore Romano* (English edition), N. 47 (1769), 20 November 2002, n° 5

The Church, not simply the bishops, but all Catholics and in particular those actively involved in public life, have a common interest with those seeking a more secularist approach to society in their concern for the dignity of the human person in society. For too long it has been accepted that religion is a matter for the bishops, and that lay Catholics in the arena of political debate are led simply by their political allegiances. Morality has been seen as a religious issue and of little if any consequence in the political world. This has to change, but the change has to be properly focused on the dignity of the person. In a special way those Catholic laity who are involved in different political and social organisations, guided by the teachings of the Church, are to endeavour to bring the truth of the Gospel into the dialogue of society.

No society can survive without a common language and a willingness to dialogue. This willingness is surely the very basis of a pluralistic society. The Church can see herself as an interested social partner who has something of value to add to the humanising of society. Unlike other pressure groups, however, she speaks to this dialogue, not to have her own agenda forwarded, but rather out of care for the dignity of the person and the State. It is the decision of the political class to listen or not to the Christian perspective. The Church has no desire to impose her will on political society by force or intimidation.

Those who fear the presence of the Church in public debate must be assisted to accept the renewed theology of the Church in relation to her commitment to political society. If in the past the Church refused public open debate, let not those of a secular disposition now return the favour in the same way. Let them ask themselves whether Christianity has any insights which could help in the ordering of society. People may not agree, but in the name of tolerance one cannot be intolerant. The Irish journalist Fintan O'Toole is aware of the positive role the Church can play in society, if she is prepared to be a partner and the others are prepared to allow her to. 'If Catholics can bring the tradition of Christian morality to bear on their society, rather than be content with a bleak reiteration of the incomprehensible into the void, then they have a real moral agenda to offer to a secularised society. And if the secular liberals can see that the minimalism of their own morality, which is a morality of the older tolerable coexistence rather than for changing things for the better, has useful things to learn from the larger ambitions of the older tradition, then there are at least grounds for dialogue'.[33]

If the Church in Ireland is to be true to the vision of Vatican II and offer Irish society the true Christian message, not of domination but of guidance and grace, then the Gospel must be preached with honest and integrity. Paul VI pointed out that our contemporaries 'listen more willingly to witnesses than to teachers, and if they do listen to teachers, it is because they are also witnesses'.[34] The Church will not be listened to by society if she is not seen to be a true follower of Christ. As is right and fitting for the Church, Christ is the key. Fundamentally her mission is not temporal; it has a primary eschatological thrust, mindful that, as the Second Vatican Council pointed out, our hope for the celestial city spurs us on to strive to build an earthly terrestrial city worthy of human fulfillment. 'The Church should see herself as the guardian of man's moral freedom and the integrity of his conscience, which is a kind of ideal space which the person needs if he is to grow as a moral being'.[35] As Yves Congar said at the time of the Council we must learn to relate all things to the Last Things[36], that is to say our hope must be in the Risen Christ who has overcome the world, and by so doing saved it. The Church in Ireland must concentrate on her spiritual mission and her primary commitment to evangelisation. What is called for now is not an unquestioning Church, nor a doubting Church, but a believing Church, dare I say a holy Church.

The call to holiness is not the Church in Ireland admitting defeat in the face of secularism's onslaught. It is not a running into the sacristy because life has become too dangerous in the marketplace of public opinion. Rather it is the Church accepting her true role in

33 Fintan O'Toole, *Black Hole, Green Card: The Disappearance of Ireland*, Dublin, New Island Books, 1994, pp. 148-149

34 Paul VI, Apostolic Exhortation *Evangelii nuntiandi* (8 December 1975), n° 41 (*Acta Apostolicae Sedis* 68 (1976), p. 31)

35 Fergal O'Connor, 'Church and State', *The Furrow* 30 (1979), p.779

36 Yves Congar, 'The Role of the Church in the Modern World', in Herbert Vorgrimler, ed., *Commentary on the Documents of Vatican II* Volume V, London/New York: Burns & Oates / Herder & Herder, 1969, p. 211

the world. The great call of Vatican II was the universal call to holiness. 'As the ... Council has vigorously re-asserted, the real mission of the Church is to bring the world back to God, to make it conscious of him as the supreme, adorable reality and its own highest good ... it is by far the most urgent, the direst need of our time, to make people aware of God. And it is the fundamental requirement for the renewal of the Church itself'.[37] This call to authentic holiness involves also a call to true citizenship. If one is true to the insights of Aquinas, it is clear that the law cannot *impose* morality. True morality comes from within; external conformity means little. The Christian seeks the salvation of souls, not that of the State. It is the person that receives the message of Christ and is redeemed in faith, not organisations. Only secondly does the believing Christian influence the organisation of society. The Church is not worried about being accepted in the marketplace of public opinion. Her only interest in the public domain is moral, 'respect for persons, care for their welfare, concern to create a community and institutions which make human development possible'.[38] And she can do this best by being first and foremost faithful to and united with her Lord. Her mission is fundamentally theological, not sociological, religious, not political.

The task for committed democrats is a difficult one. They must aim to ensure the proper ordering of society for the good of its citizens allowing for the protection and flourishing of a true and authentic democracy. The question is not how belief in God can be compatible with democracy but rather 'whether democracy can long endure if it ignores the truth about the human person?'[39] The Church believes that she can assist in this task. The challenge to modern Irish society is to allow the space in which this can be done. It is for the Church to accept the willingness of others to listen, in their common concern for the good of the person, who – the Church believes – is made in the image of God.

37 Anselm Moynihan, *The Presence of God*, Dublin, St Martin Apostolate, p. 9
38 Vincent McNamara, 'Law and Morality', *The Furrow*, 30 (1979), p. 675
39 Henry J. Hyde, 'Catholics in Politics. Reflections on a Vatican Statement', *America* Vol. 188, N° 5, Whole N° 4599, 17 February 2003. p. 8

THE CONTRIBUTORS

VIVIAN BOLAND has lectured at Tallaght, the Milltown Institute in Dublin and the Roehampton Institute in London. He is currently Senior Lecturer in Theology at St Mary's College, Strawberry Hill, Twickenham, lecturer and tutor at Blackfriars, Oxford, and Master of Students of the English Dominican Province. Author of *Ideas in God According to Saint Thomas Aquinas* (1996), he contributes frequently to theological and pastoral journals.

THOMAS BRODIE studies literary connections between the Old Testament and the New, including the partial modelling of the gospels on the Elijah-Elisha narrative and the epistles' modelling of Paul on Moses. This largely unexplored field may have considerable historical and theological implications. Director of the new Dominican Biblical Centre in Limerick, his most recent book is *The Birthing of the New Testament* (Phoenix Press, Sheffield, 2004).

ARCHIE CONLETH BYRNE taught in Tallaght and Cork: he was Regent of Studies of the Province of Ireland for six years to 1985. Though his initial teaching experience was in philosophy (logic) and dogmatics, he later specialised in Moral Theology. For his doctorate in Fribourg (Switzerland) he researched Aquinas's teaching on Angelic Knowledge. He has written many articles on moral topics.

JAMES P DONLEAVY, having done most of his studies in Tallaght, completed his theology in Rome. Later he studied Speech and Drama at the London College of Music and College of Dramatic Art. Since then his life has been spent preaching retreats and missions at home and far away. He has published numerous homilies, as well as many articles on preaching.

PHILIP GLEESON teaches theology in the Dominican Studium and the Milltown Institute, both in Dublin, and the Priory Institute, Tallaght. His most recent publication is a contribution to Leonard E. Boyle, OP, *et al.* (edd.), *Aux origines de la liturgie dominicaine* (Paris: CNRS Editions, 2004).

WILFRID J HARRINGTON was appointed Lector at the Dominican House of Studies in 1957 and is currently lecturing at the Priory Institute, at the Milltown Institute and the Church of Ireland Theological College, Dublin. Wilfrid has taught summer courses in the United States annually since 1965 and is the author of 48 books, among the most recent being *Seeking Spiritual Growth through the Bible* (Paulist Press).

JOHN HARRIS studied philosophy and politics in UCD. He lectured in theology in Tallaght in the 1990s. The title of his recent doctoral thesis was 'Ethics in Constitutional Law: a theological reflection on the preamble to the Irish Constitution'. He is currently Moderator of the Studium in Dublin.

BENEDICT HEGARTY taught Fundamental Theology in Tallaght from 1967 to 1979 and was Regent of Studies from 1973 to 1979. He has taught Scripture at the *Mater Dei* Institute, Clonliffe and All Hallows' Colleges, and lectured on Ecumenical Studies at Milltown and Kimmage Manor, all in Dublin. He is currently a chaplain in Tallaght Hospital and is curate in St Dominic's parish, Tallaght.

JOSEPH KAVANAGH lived in Trinidad & Tobago from 1969 to 1999 (apart from two three-year stints in Ireland), and worked in various Trinidadian parishes, as well as teaching in the regional seminary. He has been Moderator of The Priory Institute in Tallaght since 2000.

JEROME MURPHY-O'CONNOR has been Professor of New Testament at Jerusalem's *Ecole Biblique* since 1967. His research has focussed on the historical background of the NT, and he has published extensively on the apostle Paul and on the historical Jesus. His most recent book, *Jesus and Paul: Parallel Lives*, combines these two interests.

PAUL MURRAY teaches at Rome's Angelicum University on the literature of the mystical tradition. Apart from four books of poetry, his other publications include: *T.S. Eliot and Mysticism: The Secret History of Four Quartets*; and, most recently, *The New Wine of Dominican Spirituality: A Drink Called Happiness*.

GERARD J NORTON is Director of the Retreat House at Tallaght, where he reflects on the word of God with all comers. He writes on the ancient history of transmission of the Hebrew and Greek Psalters. Gerard returned to Tallaght in 2002 after having been senior lecturer at the University of Birmingham, and previous posts at Trinity College, Dublin, and the *Ecole Biblique*, Jerusalem.

DONAGH O'SHEA taught philosophy and logic in Tallaght 1972-1977, and since then has been involved in retreat work at home and abroad. He is a member of the St Mary's Community in Cork, and provides content for the website of www.goodnews.ie

LIAM G WALSH studied, after Tallaght, at *le Saulchoir* (Paris) and the Angelicum University (Rome). He taught theology in Tallaght, in the Angelicum and at the University of Fribourg, Switzerland. He has been Regent of Studies of the Dominican Province of Ireland since 2000. He writes and lectures, and teaches the course on Fundamental Theology, at the Studium in St Saviour's, Dublin.